THE WAY
Success
works

HOW TO DECIDE, BELIEVE, AND
BEGIN TO LIVE YOUR BEST LIFE

BY JOAN POSIVY

GLOBAL youth PROJECT.ORG

Printed in Canada, 2015

PRAISE FOR
THE WAY SUCCESS WORKS

"If you ever get the feeling that you could be living your life in a greater and grander way, do yourself, your community, and the planet a favor and buy this book. As Joan suggests, your magnificent future awaits!"
Jack Canfield, Coauthor of The Success Principles: How to Get from Where You Are to Where You Want to Be™

"This book is extremely well written and dense with information. It has the potential to change lives and broaden young people's thinking in a radical, revolutionary way."
Sigrid Macdonald, Bestselling Author of Getting Hip

"The skilful blend of engaging stories and valuable examples put forward by Joan in The Way Success Works is the result of her passionate understanding of the creative mind we all possess. There is no doubt that this gem will be an inspiration for youth across all cultures."
Jean-René Leduc, Chief Instructor for Canada: Aikido Kenkyukai International

"This is a recipe for success. I highly recommend this book to youth and anyone looking to support a youth on their way to success."
Daniel Moores, CEC

MORE PRAISE FOR *THE WAY SUCCESS WORKS*

"After reading *The Way Success Works*, you'll begin to take your dreams very seriously. If you walk the path laid out in this insightful and inspiring book, you can't help but succeed! The book expands on the outstanding work Joan has done with Rotary sponsored Leadership Programs like RYLA, which has made a difference in the lives of countless young adults – see what it will do for you!"
Dave Douglas, Author of Leading the Way: A Step-by-Step Guide to Discovering and Building Your Leadership Skills

"With a fresh take on the principles of success, you will be blessed with an empowering, kind-hearted, and encouraging formula for success in living your best life."
Peggy McColl, New York Times Bestselling Author

"I've known Joan for more than 20 years. Her message to young people with the Global Youth Project is one that is desperately needed... I would encourage you to share this book with your children, your grandchildren, your nieces and nephews and your neighbours. Give the book as a birthday gift; give several copies to a school library in another country – spread the word: this is *The Way Success Works!*"
Marilyn Strong, speaker, entrepreneur and bestselling author of Getting Paid to Pay Attention

Copyright © 2015 Joan Posivy. All rights reserved.

Published by Global Youth Project Inc.
4691A Hwy 3A, Nelson, BC Canada V1L 6M6

No part of this publication may be reproduced, stored in a retrieval system, or transmitted in any form by any process – electronic, photocopying, recording, or otherwise – without the prior written consent of Global Youth Project Inc.

This publication is designed to provide accurate and authoritative information in regard to the subject matter covered. It is sold with the understanding that neither the publisher nor author is engaged in rendering legal, accounting, financial, medical or other professional advice. If expert assistance is required, the services of a competent professional should be sought. In the event you use any of the information in this book for yourself, the author and the publisher assume no responsibility for your actions.

While the author has made every effort to provide accurate website addresses and contact information at the time of publication, neither the publisher nor the author assumes any responsibility for errors or for changes that occur after publication. Further, neither the author nor publisher has any control over, and does not assume any responsibility for, third-party websites or their content.

The views of the author may not necessarily represent those of the youth interviewed.

Designed by Ayva Cowell
Cover illustration by Giorgio Angiolini
Licensed by RHS, Lindley Library, UK

ISBN 978-0-9948360-0-7

Printed in Canada

Dedicated to you who have the courage to pursue your dreams.
May these pages support your journey.

FOREWORD

I'VE BEEN WAITING FOR THIS BOOK. 25 years ago, I told the author she should write one. I even suggested a title: *The Persistent Woman*. Joan earned that moniker back then by being one of our most successful facilitators in North America of my video program, *You Were Born Rich*. When other facilitators would call her for advice to ask her what she was doing, her answer was simple: every day she was working at being a "product of the product."

What Joan understands and teaches is that it's not enough to simply have an intellectual understanding of universal law and principles of success. For your results to improve, you must step out, act on, and apply what you've learned. This is where most people stumble. It's not that they lack the potential or capability to live the life of their dreams; each one of us has deep reservoirs of talent and ability within us. What is often missing, though, is the understanding of why we don't act on what we know.

The results that you are getting in life – your happiness, health, and wealth – are rooted in your actions; they're tied to what you do and what you don't do, to the opportunities you seize or those you let pass by. Whether or not you are aware of it, these everyday choices you make are guided by your paradigm – the collection of beliefs and habits deep in your subconscious mind that direct every move you make. These paradigms affect what you eat, the way you talk, and even the way you walk. They govern your time management, ability to earn money, your logic… your successes and your failures.

In these pages, Joan will share with you not only how she has altered her own paradigms again and again to achieve success, but more importantly, she'll show you precisely how you too can affect tremendous change in your own life. Realize, you have the ability to achieve any goal you seriously desire.

What makes this book so unique is that Joan doesn't just detail her own proven, time-tested blueprint for goal achievement. Nor is it simply a collection of inspirational stories about amazing youth from around the world. It's not even just a sharing of her successes, the principles behind which she'll show you that anyone could emulate. Rather, it's an intricately woven tapestry of all these elements.

This is no ordinary book. You'll likely be drawn to read it cover to cover the first time around. And, though you can't help but be inspired by the youth and their stories, make sure you take full advantage of the wealth of information, ideas, and understanding within these pages by going back to each chapter to study and incorporate these winning strategies into your own life. If you do so, you will be richly rewarded.

In October of 2014, in celebration of the 25th anniversary of the filming of *You Were Born Rich*, Joan attended the seminar I was presenting in Los Angeles. She shared with me her vision for the Global Youth Project and, in particular, her vision for this book... which I wholeheartedly encouraged. And while it's her passion to be working with and championing youth around the globe, I can assure you the information Joan shares in this book will benefit readers of any age.

This woman practices what she preaches. Devour this book, and follow her advice to the letter. Know that you are in very good hands.

Bob Proctor
Featured teacher in The Secret
International best-selling author of You Were Born Rich

CONTENTS

Foreword .... ix // Introduction xv

ACT I: DECIDE

Chapter 1 .... *The Good News (3)*
- » THE TRUTH ABOUT YOU
- » YOUR CO-CREATIVE ABILITY
- » DON'T BE FOOLED
- » YOU WANT TO DO WHAT? (TIM'S STORY)
- » THE TIME IS NOW
- » WE CAN SOLVE THAT! THE SUNCAYR SOLUTION

Chapter 2 .... *Dreaming Big (15)*
- » THE ULTIMATE DIY PROJECT: BUILD YOUR IMAGE
- » IT'S YOUR LIFE. WHAT WILL YOU MAKE OF IT?
- » DREAM BIG, START SMALL: CAMERON'S LESSON
- » DESIGNING YOUR LIFE: 4 PRIMARY QUESTIONS
- » DREAMS EXCEEDED: NICK & SWEETGRASS...
- » YOUR LIST OF 100
- » CAPTAIN YOUR OWN SHIP

Chapter 3 .... *Decision Time (35)*
- » BRINGING YOUR GOALS TO LIFE
- » THE POWER OF THE VISION BOARD
- » SHARING (OR NOT) YOUR GOALS
- » DEEP & A LIFESAVING IDEA
- » SO HAVE YOU DECIDED? ARE YOU IN?

ACT II: BELIEVE

Chapter 4 .... *The State of Mind... It Must Be Belief* (53)
- FROM LOCAL TO GLOBAL: FRASER'S SUPERJAM
- THE GRAND DEBATE: NATURE & NURTURE
- CHOOSING YOUR PATH: TUGI'S MISSION
- PUTING AN END TO MENTAL MALPRACTICE
- WELCOME TO THE PANIC ZONE!
- I'VE GOT $100 IN MY POCKET
- EXPANDING YOUR COMFORT ZONE

Chapter 5 .... *New Habits. New You. New Results.* (77)
- THE COMPANY YOU KEEP
- PERSISTENCE PAYS: ZACHARY'S TALE

Chapter 6 .... *Hold It In Your Head, Hold It In Your Hand* (85)
- THE CREATIVE PROCESS
- FROM DREAMING TO MANIFESTING: 7 STEPS
- VISUALIZATION & ATTRACTION
- KEEP GROWING YOUR VISION
- THE POWER OF A SINGLE THOUGHT

Chapter 7 .... *Take Control Of Your Thinking (And Your Life!)* (96)
- SET LIMITS
- BE INTROSPECTIVE
- THE CONSEQUENCE OF BLAMING OTHERS
- LIGHTENING YOUR MENTAL LOAD
- THE TWO MOST DESTRUCTIVE EMOTIONS
- TIME IS A GIFT: BE HERE NOW
- THAT WAS YESTERDAY
- YOUR MAGNIFICENT FUTURE AWAITS

ACT III: BEGIN

Chapter 8 .... *Get By With A Little Help From Your Friends* (114)
- ⇛ EXPERIENCED MENTORS: NOT OPTIONAL!
- ⇛ IF YOU DON'T ASK, YOU'LL NEVER KNOW
- ⇛ ACCOUNTABILITY PARTNERS
- ⇛ STRENGTH IN NUMBERS: MASTERMIND ALLIANCES

Chapter 9 .... *The Universe Only Knows How To Say Yes* (123)
- ⇛ EMPOWERED EVENINGS
- ⇛ THE HUG SEEN AROUND THE WORLD
- ⇛ MINDFUL MORNINGS

Chapter 10 .... *Cultivate Habits Of Success* (129)
- ⇛ YOUR HIGHEST ROI: SELF IMPROVEMENT
- ⇛ THE HUMAN ELEMENT
- ⇛ MAKING QUANTUM LEAPS IN PRODUCTIVITY
- ⇛ FAST-TRACK YOUR SUCCESS
- ⇛ APPRECIATION FOR WINNING (AND LOSING)
- ⇛ PERSISTENCE
- ⇛ GRATITUDE
- ⇛ WHEN TO START? TODAY IS GOOD!

Chapter 11 .... *It's a Wrap* (145)

Conclusion .... *Now Is Your Time To Shine* (149)

Acknowledgements (151)
Meet Our Featured Youth (155)
About The Author & Global Youth Project (157)

INTRODUCTION

IT WAS DECISION TIME. At the age of 19, I found myself standing in the hallway of an airport hotel on Dixon Road in Toronto, Canada. Little did I know then, I was about to make a choice that would significantly impact the rest of my life. "It's such a huge cost," I remember saying to my boyfriend, Karl. "We don't have that kind of money to spare."

"Yeah, I get that," he shrugged. "But do you think it'll help you?"

"Absolutely," I replied. It was true. I knew – really, truly, deeply – that it would. And I think Karl knew it too. But regardless, there was an all-too-common inner struggle happening for me that day. On one hand, it felt like my instinct was rooting for me to go for it, but my thinking brain kept dragging me back to the money thing.

I was wavering over the decision to sign up for a personal development training program at a cost of $350 (which, at the time, felt like a fortune). And even if I were able to come up with the funds to attend, could this really help *me* – the introverted one? Could it give me the gift of shedding my skin of shyness to become outgoing and social? It would have been so much easier (and cheaper) to just walk away and forget about it. It would probably be a waste of time and money anyway, I told myself. You can't change who you are. Or can you? It's that possibility that kept me from walking out. After all, who else was there to take responsibility for my life, other than me?

Sometimes, the best choice is the fly-by-the-seat-of-your-pants one, and it definitely was that night. "What the hell?" I said. I committed.

In my eyes, it was a huge investment, but what I received in return was priceless. Bob Proctor, the person leading the course, managed to convince me that I could essentially have, do, or be anything

I truly desired. Imagine that! No wonder I was drawn to the material. And it wasn't because I was anyone special or out of the ordinary. This, he told me, *applied to everyone*. If I was willing to put in the time to study, learn, and apply what I was learning, he said, I would certainly see wonderful results. As it turns out, he was right. The more I studied the power of the mind and human potential, the more I came to believe that what I was learning was indeed true. Through applying those lessons, and others I picked up along the way, I owned my first house within the year – I was still just 19. I had started to seriously let go of all the reasons why I couldn't do something and instead focus on all the ways I could. It's amazing the options that we begin to see when our thinking is properly aligned with the good that we desire.

After receiving a few promotions, I was appointed branch manager of a financial institution at 22 years old: at the time, the youngest person in Canada to ever have done so.

Reality check. The results I was getting made me step back and take a look at what I was learning and applying. I could come to no other conclusion than the obvious (if seemingly unbelievable) one: these ideas work. Up until that day in the hotel, I had only studied standard academic subjects: math, science, history and so on. This was the first time anyone had ever talked to me about my mind and my potential. As a result, I had grown up to think – incorrectly – that when you were born, you were dealt certain cards (your circumstances, traits, characteristics and talents). These cards were simply what you had to play with for the rest of your life. But what if you were dealt a weak hand?

Soon enough, I discovered that you can *choose* your hand. You can throw cards back, pick new ones, and shuffle the deck. There is a process, of course, and it takes discipline, courage, and a large dose of persistence and perseverance... but it is *definitely* possible and more than definitely worthwhile. I'm so grateful to have realized that possibility, and since I began to absorb these teachings, my life has been a rich tapestry of adventure, travel, unique experiences, and incredible pursuits. And I can trace the path of success back to its origin – to the single decision I made that night in Toronto. Today, it's decision time for you. It's your life. What are you going to do with it?

I hope you have plans to make the rest of your life an epic journey. Regardless of your present circumstances, it is most certainly possible. If you are not absolutely convinced of your ability to live your heart's desire or, perhaps, not quite sure what your destiny might be, I encourage you to journey with me through the pages of this book.

By the time we're done, you'll have the tools to:
1. Decide your destiny,
2. Believe you can manifest your heart's desire, and
3. Begin your first steps.

In addition to discovering tested strategies and techniques that I've used and made work, you'll hear from a number of youth around the world who are marvellous examples of living the life of their wildest dreams. Together, we're on a mission to provide you with the tools to create a rich, abundant, and fulfilling life of your own.

In each case, these young people saw a problem to solve or an opportunity to make the world a better place for us all, and rather than accept things as they were, they decided to step up. And so can you. They may speak different languages and embrace different customs, but these youth all share the desire to create tangible change in their lives and the lives of others. Does this sound like you?

The principles that they are using (consciously or otherwise) are universal and available to us all. Just like them, you have an incredible stockpile of talent and potential within you waiting to be expressed to the world. I can say that without having met you because, regardless of your age, the country you find yourself in, or our cultural differences, we are all connected to the same source.

When I founded the Global Youth Project (www.globalyouthproject.org) the emphasis was (and will continue to be) on our international community of youth. Today, you and I have at our fingertips the ability to collaborate with and learn from each other more than any other generation alive in the history of civilization. There are incredible youth out there who are tapping into their deep resources of talent and ability to make the world a better place for us all. Until now, you may have had only a glimpse of what you are truly capable of. While we all have the same inherent ability to tap into the infinite source of supply, the way we express that in our lives and the gifts we bring to the world are unique to each of us. ***No one else can make the contribution that you can.*** Now is your time to shine. The world needs you. Get ready to amaze yourself.

ACT ONE

DECIDE

CHAPTER ONE

THE GOOD NEWS

"Anything's possible if you've got enough nerve."
J.K. Rowling, Novelist

How often do we identify a problem – on a personal, local, national or even global scale – and simply pass it by? We so often accept the story of: *that's just the way it is.* Thankfully (for ourselves and for our planet), there is a whole generation of youth today awakening to the potential within themselves to put on the brakes and re-write the story. "Hey, wait a minute!" they're starting to say. "There's something I can do about this." Though support of friends, family, and community cannot be understated, it (whatever *it* may be) begins with a single person's single thought. And that's where it all begins for you too: in your very own marvellous mind.

THE TRUTH ABOUT YOU

You have, without a doubt, *deep* reservoirs of talent and ability within you. Sometimes they just need a little… uncovering. Let me explain. After hearing speaker Jack Canfield once tell the story of Thailand's Golden

Buddha, I immediately added a visit there to my list of goals. Since we never really know quite how our goals will materialize, it was exciting to imagine how I might end up in Thailand. A few years later, the opportunity presented itself when I was invited by Bob Proctor to join him in Kuala Lumpur and co-present a seminar for Malaysian Airlines. Given that the airline flies worldwide, there were employees in attendance from all over the world… including Thailand! During the course of those few days, an attendee based in Bangkok invited me to join her there for a visit after the seminar. Perfect!

This was clearly my chance to visit the Golden Buddha, a statue housed in the temple of Wat Traimit. So what was the draw? This three metre tall, five-tonne Buddha is crafted of solid gold, and is thought to be roughly seven centuries old. Its estimated value is $250 million. But the most intriguing part of its story is surely that for most of its life, the magnificent piece was shrouded in false layers. A long, long time ago, when facing the threat of invasion by Burmese soldiers, those close to the statue covered it with a heavy coat of plaster, which was painted and inlaid with bits of coloured glass. And as such it remained, hidden in broad daylight, and its true value eventually forgotten… until 1955.

It was then, as the piece was being moved to a new location in Bangkok, that it was lifted from its pedestal; the ropes broke, and the statue smashed to the ground. As it did, some of the plaster broke off… revealing the beauty and value of the gold beneath. And it is indeed beautiful. Finally in Thailand, staring in awe at the Buddha and considering its history, I found it hard to imagine that something so commanding, so stunning, could have remained hidden so long.

Do you see the moral here? The very same awe can – and should – be felt for what lies at the core of you and me. We, like the storied Buddha, are born golden! Almost immediately, though, we begin to collect layers of negative conditioning, feelings of lack and inadequacy, and all sorts of limiting beliefs. These pile up over time and shroud the brightness that is our true way of being – our genuine beauty and presence. For too many individuals, those layers are never cracked or peeled away. They simply keep building, thickening, hiding, over a lifetime.

> *My genuine hope is that as you contemplate and work with the stories and ideas in these pages, together we can chip away at the layers that have been preventing you from seeing clearly the immense potential that is your true self.*

Earl Nightingale, co-founder of the Nightingale-Conant Corporation (and mentor to Bob), made an interesting and accurate observation. "Right here we come to a rather strange fact," he said. "We tend to minimize the things we can do, the goals we can accomplish, and for some equally strange reason, we think other people can do things that we cannot. That's not true. I want you to realize that you have deep reservoirs of talent and ability within you."

YOUR CO-CREATIVE ABILITY

Both science and theology tell us that the universe is a closed system. Energy cannot be created or destroyed; it merely changes form. One of those forms, of course, is matter, and matter is in a constant state of either *creation* (we call that growth) or its polar opposite, *decay*. And what does this have to do with your future results? Everything.

Because most people go through their life focused on the wrong end of the creative process, they are often frustrated trying desperately to improve their results. The change – the choice, if you will – needs to be made at the source. Imagine you were to plant a seed in the ground and mindfully nurture it. Say an orange seed. Eventually, it would grow into an orange tree. Not a pine tree or a maple tree or an oak tree – only an orange tree. Why? Because residing within that seed is an embryo – *a plan* – that dictates what it can grow into. It can't grow into anything else.

If you were to dissect the seed and study it under the most powerful microscope, you'd never see an orange tree in there. Why? Because it's not there. There's only the plan. Once planted, the seed attracts everything that is in harmony with its vibratory rate within the ground, and eventually when it breaks through the surface, it attracts from the atmosphere.

Guess what? You and I also have a plan that we're constantly growing into. A HUGE difference, though, between us and the seed, is that we CHOOSE what we will become. We create the plan! Whether or not a person makes these choices consciously and purposefully, of course, is entirely another matter. But the exciting part – the real sense of freedom and no-limit achievement in our lives – comes from the understanding that we CAN create a magnificent plan for ourselves and execute our plan with joy, and love, and positive expectations.

Are there challenges, setbacks, and obstacles along the way? Absolutely. Most of us were not raised in an environment that nurtures no-limit thinking. So we set a goal of something we would like to have, do, or be. Done properly, this is like planting the seed. We get excited about what it will be like once we have reached our target. But then, when we don't see it happening right away, we become full of fear, doubt, and anxiety, and we've just uprooted that beautiful seed of an idea we planted.

And again, we start attracting more of what we say we don't want. But it doesn't have to be that way. The more we study and discover about our self – our true self – and learn to tap into our higher nature, the less time we spend in a state of doubt, fear, and anxiety.

I'm aware that there are some people out there in the world who do not believe this to be true. They believe only in what they can see, and see immediately. I'd like to challenge that belief for them when they are standing amid a hurricane. Can you and I see the raging wind? Of course not. We can see only its effects. Just like this, the results that you see in your life right now are the effects of the happenings of your mind. Our external results are merely a reflection of our internal reality. And that, in a nutshell, is why all this is so important.

The absence of evidence is not the evidence of absence.
Carl Sagan, Cosmos

DON'T BE FOOLED

In addition to the new insights and ideas you'll pick up as you make your way through this book, it's quite likely that you'll come across ideas you've heard before. That's when your thought process is likely to kick in and tell you: "Yeah, yeah. I already know that." I've been guilty of this far too often in the past. The danger is that we can *know* something, but knowledge alone won't bring about the significant life changes we desperately crave. We can trick ourselves into thinking we're pretty familiar with a concept because we've read about it, talked about it, or heard about it somewhere. Unless we've totally integrated it, though – unless we're living it and it's part of who we are – we can't truly *know* it.

It's fascinating to me that today, it takes mere seconds to send an idea across the globe. Text, email, tweet, or post it, and it's arrived. A long distance but a short time. Yet for an idea to travel from our head to our heart (from concept to real integration), it can take much longer. Days, weeks, even years. A short distance but a long time.

Take, for example, a person who sets the goal of getting into better physical shape. In order to do that, they know rationally the steps they have to take; they need to improve their diet, exercise more, get enough sleep, and so on and so forth. But, as so many of us have come to realize, this sort of knowing simply isn't enough. You'll see in the coming sections that I stand strongly behind creating and using a vision board. When used correctly, it can be a phenomenal tool on the journey of achieving that which you most desire. And for most of us, it's actually essential. Do you have one? Are you using it? If not, while you're studying this book, you'll want to start one. It's a step in the right direction… in the direction of action.

Years ago, shortly before I would be speaking to an audience of aspiring young entrepreneurs, I had the opportunity to sit down with Carl-Johan Bonnier, Chairman of the Board of The Bonnier Group (a privately held Swedish media group of 175 companies operating in 16 countries). "If you were to be standing in front of that group," I asked him, "what advice would you give them?"

He replied without hesitation. "I'd tell them to take action," he said. Bonnier went on to explain that over his decades in business, he had met countless people with fantastic ideas who too often didn't take that critical next step: the step of action. If you read about an idea here that inspires or resonates with you, don't wait. Act. **Now.**

YOU WANT TO DO WHAT? (TIM'S STORY)

"I want to own my own restaurant," Tim announced. While his father had always been very supportive of Tim, at that moment, he was trying to suppress his doubts. Not only was Tim just 14 years old, his father, Keith, had never heard of anyone with Tim's medical condition – Down Syndrome – owning a restaurant. As time and events unfolded, though, both Keith and his wife, Jeannie, had to start taking their son seriously. During high school, he was doing quite well working part-time at a local restaurant. So much so that one day, Tim's manager mentioned it to Keith. "We can track an increase in revenue during the weekends that Tim works," he said.

Keith had to admit that customers were simply drawn to his spirit. "People would phone the restaurant and ask, 'Is Tim on shift tonight?'"

It got his parents thinking. If Tim was creating that kind of economic impact for the restaurant at which he worked, maybe that charisma could be harnessed for his own benefit. Tim always had a knack for connecting with people. He was elected homecoming king by the highest margin of votes in his high school's history, and, during graduation week, Tim was voted Student of the Year by the faculty and staff.

Before becoming a full-time restaurateur, though, Tim needed some skills demanded by the industry. He headed south to Eastern New Mexico University in Roswell, which offers programmes for people with intellectual disabilities. He went on to graduate with certificates in Food Service, Office Skills, and Restaurant Hosting. After some travelling with his parents and working once again for an already established restaurant, it was time for Tim to realize his dream. In October 2010, Tim's Place opened its doors. Tim was 24. "It's the place of dreams," he says with exuberance. "It was built with dreams. And I didn't let my disability get in the way of owning a restaurant. This place is awesome. It's full of love and joy and happiness."

Not surprisingly, he has adopted Walt Disney's famous quote as his motto. "If you can dream it, you can do it." When you really believe in something, magic happens.

No one had to teach Tim much about creating buzz for a new venture. About a week prior to the opening, he turned to his dad while they were working at the new location. "I'm out of business cards," he said.

"We're not open yet, Tim. What are you doing?" asked Keith, exasperated. "Where did all the cards go?"

"I'm just giving them to people." Tim shrugged.

Keith sighed. "What kind of people?"

"At the store," his son replied. "Wherever I am."

Ask a silly question… Keith launched into a fatherly lecture about the appropriate use of business cards. He went on and on about certain circumstances in which you should give those cards and how Tim would just have to learn that as he learned about business. In the midst of his rant, a car pulled up just in front of the restaurant, and six women stepped out.

"Can I help you?" Keith asked.

"We're here for breakfast," one of the women responded.

"I appreciate that, ma'am, but we're not open yet," Keith apologized. "How did you hear about us?"

"Well, I met Tim in the frozen foods section of the grocery store," she said. She held up a business card he had given her. And then Keith and Jeannie ordered Tim a LOT more business cards.

THE TIME IS NOW

We live in one of the most amazing, exciting, enlivening eras that humanity has ever experienced. Never before in the history of mankind have we had the tools at our disposal to make our dreams come true to the degree that we have now. What one day seems impossible is, the next day, our new reality.

It was only a short time ago that most of us were brand new to the idea of 3D printing, for example. Today, it's nearly a mainstream industry. Enter Nikki Kaufman. After many unsuccessful attempts at trying to find a pair of earbuds that would work well for her, Kaufman discovered that she could have a pair custom made… but she'd need to visit a doctor, invest thousands of dollars, and wait weeks for them to be manufactured. She decided instead to explore 3D printing. It's a process whereby a three-dimensional, solid object can be created from a digital file. The printer lays down successive layers of material until the entire object is created – and this is exactly the technology she needed. The idea for her company was born.

Kaufman's enterprise, *Normal*, allows you to order an affordable, comfortable pair of tailor-made premium earphones, simply by taking photos of each of your ears via a free mobile smartphone application. And Nikki and her team are just one example of one technology inspiring individuals across the globe to shape the future of manufacturing.

Today, if you can build an image in your mind of something you'd like to create, you can bet that there are the people and resources somewhere in the world able to help you do that. And now, you can literally find them at the touch of a button.

WE CAN SOLVE THAT! THE SUNCAYR SOLUTION

How often do we meet an obstacle or encounter a problem and simply resign ourselves to believing that's just the way it is? Have you ever gotten a sunburn, for example? For some people, it's a minor irritation. For others, it can lead to serious medical problems such as skin cancer.

For 20-year-old Rachel Pautler and four of her friends – all nanotechnology engineering students at the University of Waterloo in Ontario, Canada – the sunburn problem was one to solve! What began as a brainstorming session for a fourth-year design project soon became their startup company, Suncayr.

These students discovered that the issue for most people was not forgetting to wear sunscreen, but rather that it would wear off during the day without the users noticing, so it would not be reapplied.

Their solution? Use a marker they had created (just like a regular magic marker) to draw something (anything – which is part of the fun) somewhere on your skin that will be exposed to the sun's rays. It'll go on clear. Then apply your sunscreen. Go outdoors and have fun! Later in the day, as your sunscreen dissolves, it begins to lose its effectiveness, and your drawing will start to show – purple, red, orange, or yellow, depending on the marker you chose. When you see it, you know it's time to re-apply your sun protection!

It's a great idea. And apparently a lot of other people think so too. Each time I've checked in with them since we first met, the product seems to have won yet another award or competition and attracted more funding or supporters. This is serving the group well, as they are in the process of gaining approval from the North American regulatory agencies.

In my mind, each of them is already a winner. They dreamed of what could be, and they took action. Along the way, they've gained valuable insight and expertise that will serve them well in any future endeavours they decide to participate in. Even though they have the academic background, the team still faced a lot of challenges in terms of the technology as it was completely different than anything they'd ever done before. "We discovered that sunscreen actually dissolves everything," explains Rachel, "so we had to make our product sunscreen-proof, which would have obviously been a huge design flaw if we couldn't do that."

Apart from the science side of things, running a startup company requires a whole other set of expertise. But that didn't slow them down. "A big challenge has been learning how to build a business," she admits. "We're all engineers; we've got great tech backgrounds, but we had no idea how to do any sales or marketing or accounting – we had to learn a lot in a very short period of time."

Chances are you are not going to be an expert in every area that's required in your goal achievement. But that's okay, because you'll attract what and who you need! (More on that later.) The key is that you don't let *not knowing how to do something* stop you from pursuing a dream. Rachel and the rest of the team didn't know how to create the marker. It had never been done before! At least not until they came along. What would you like to create that doesn't exist today?

Consider this. The ability to create anything – say the smartphone, or the iWatch, or a sunscreen marker, for example – has always been present. Likewise, we weren't introduced to air travel in the last century because somehow the laws of nature changed. What's required, though – what brings it alive – is for someone to develop an awareness;

someone needs to come up with, recognize, and believe strongly in an idea for it to actualize. They must believe *so* strongly that in spite of how often they are told that it can't be done, or that it's a silly waste of time, they forge onward. History books are chock full of examples like this. When President Kennedy asked Dr. Wernher Von Braun (widely considered to be the father of the American space program and modern day rocket science) what it would take to build a rocket that could carry a man to the moon and bring him back safely to the Earth, Von Braun had a no-nonsense reply. "The will to do it," he said. And indeed, where there's a genuine will, there's a way.

It's time to step up, count yourself in, and start to live the life of your dreams. But first things first. What exactly does the life of your dreams look like? My heartfelt wish for you is that it's big, bold, and overwhelmingly beautiful.

CHAPTER TWO

DREAMING BIG

I have always believed in going after the things you want in life. Because there truly are no limits to what's possible.
Cameron Johnson, You Call the Shots

THE ULTIMATE DIY PROJECT: BUILD YOUR IMAGE

Everything starts with an image in your mind, including your ideal life. You need to decide what that looks like for you, and you're the only one who can do that. It's the ultimate do-it-yourself project. Take a look around you. Everything you see began as a single thought in a single mind, maybe recently, or maybe long ago. The place that you are in physically (perhaps a house, a cafe, or a library), the e-reader or the actual book you're holding, the piece of furniture you are using… all those things began with someone, somewhere. That's how everything starts. A person builds the image and then makes it happen.

All those individuals, as well as you and I, have arrived on this planet with six intellectual gifts: imagination, perception, reason, will, intuition, and memory. I'm asking you now to use your *imagination* and start to create images of your ideal future. If you already possess clearly defined goals that you are working toward, use these exercises to add layers of detail to your picture or maybe to help it grow and evolve.

Most importantly, you need to recognize that no one else can even begin to guess at what you are capable of doing, so DO NOT sell yourself short when designing your life. Too often people settle for far less than they are capable of achieving, and consequently never discover the true depths of their abilities. "If you plan on being anything less than you are capable of being," suggested psychologist Abraham Maslow, "you will probably be unhappy all the days of your life."

> Your dream has to be your dream, and no one else can have rules around that. At the end of the day, it's your life, and *you've* got to look yourself in the eye in 20 years.
>
> **Zachary Rook, Your Local Movers, Australia**

IT'S YOUR LIFE. WHAT WILL YOU MAKE OF IT?

Every day, you trade every moment, every breath, for *something*. What are you trading for? Our time is so incredibly short that it would be a shame to waste it thinking about what could have been. **Now is the time. Wherever you are is the place. Decide. Believe. Begin.**

It is absolutely essential that you do not let your present circumstances dictate the vision you craft of your ultimate future. Know, without judgment, that your present circumstances are simply the result of your thinking, your decisions, and your actions up until now. If you want to create for yourself a more expansive, rewarding, and exciting life, you need to engage with your imagination; it's the gift that allows us to dream of what could be. The same Bob Proctor who unknowingly helped me fulfill my goal of visiting Thailand's Golden Buddha (and who contributed so markedly to, among countless other projects, mega-bestseller *The Secret*) often speaks of the tendency we have to limit our dreams. "We've been conditioned to live from the outside-in rather than the inside-out," he points out. "It's one of the reasons too many people are not living the kind of life they are capable of. They make the all-too-common mistake of looking at their present circumstances – their bank account, their connections, their past accomplishments and failures and, based on that, they decide their plans for the future, if at all. That is a sure recipe for simply creating more of the same. We've got to stop doing that."

The key is to delve into your imagination. Get in there, and in doing so, quiet the swirling thoughts about your present circumstances. Ask, really truthfully, what you would like to have, do, or be. Do not be concerned, yet, about HOW you will create your successes. For the moment, focus only on what you want them to be. The rest can come later.

Before you begin, let me share with you a word of caution. It's almost a guarantee that if you really open up and dream about what could be possible for you, you'll soon enough encounter some internal resistance. You know the voice well, I'm sure. We all do. "You can't do that," it says. "You don't have enough ____ (fill in the blank: money, smarts, experience, contacts). You'll never make it work." So how do you handle that? Treat it gently but firmly. Imagine it's a sweet but untrained puppy. No one has yet taken the time, so you'll need to train it. Acknowledge it, and give it some direction. "I hear you," you could say, "but I'm busy right now. Go lie down and be quiet." And then continue. Just like a puppy, you'll likely have to tell it again and again… and again. And just like a puppy, with the right guidance, it will learn… eventually. Be patient.

DREAM BIG, START SMALL: CAMERON'S LESSON

Cameron Johnson started his first business at the age of nine with $50 and a home computer. He went on to become one of the most successful young entrepreneurs in the world, having started nearly a dozen profitable businesses and making his first million before graduating high school. By the age of 19, he'd already been offered – and turned down – an offer of $10 million in venture capital because he didn't feel comfortable with the conditions attached.

When I asked Cameron for the most important piece of advice he felt he could share with you, he felt very strongly about two things. The first, just like the advice from Carl-Johan Bonnier, was to *take action*. The second, he insisted, was to *really put yourself out there.*

Cameron first learned the value of both these things shortly after his eighth birthday. He had just watched *Home Alone 2: Lost in New York*, much of which was shot in Donald Trump's Plaza Hotel in New York City. He decided he just had to see Manhattan for himself and pleaded with his parents to take him. His dad made him a deal. "You get straight A's, and I'll take you to New York." He did. And his parents kept their end of the bargain. But Cameron had one more request. He wanted to stay at The Plaza. Lucky kid… they agreed.

Unbeknown to his parents, eight-year-old Cameron set about writing a letter to Donald Trump, explaining that he and his family would be in New York and asking him if he could please see the suite where they filmed the movie. He never received a reply.

When the day arrived, Cameron and his parents flew to New York and walked through the lobby of The Plaza to check in. His parents were shocked when the woman checking them in leaned over the counter toward the young boy. "Are you Cameron Johnson?" she asked. He nodded. Not only had Trump received the letter, he had arranged for the family to receive a number of special gifts – the biggest and most impressive of which was that he had upgraded their room at no cost. Cameron would not only *see* the suite where the movie was filmed… the family would stay in that very suite for the length of their visit to New York.

"That whole experience at The Plaza taught me how important it is to go after what you want," says Cameron. "There was no real reason why my parents and I should have been treated so well. We weren't VIPs or connected to Trump or the Trump organization in any way." So why then? Because he wrote him and asked!

That first business at the age of nine? It was a greeting card company that he started after getting his first computer. Together with his dad, Cameron came up with the name *Cheers & Tears Printing Company*. "Talk about starting small," he laughs. "It doesn't get much smaller. But *I was already dreaming big*. And though (it) was a tiny operation, I learned a great deal from that little business that I've applied to all my businesses ever since."

This tiny operation is one of the reasons I love Cameron's story; it proves that you can start a project from next to nothing and grow it into something. And he didn't just do it once. He's done it over and over and over again.

Not only was he already dreaming big from a young age, he was unknowingly using the power of visualization. "I imagined myself in a big office, answering a phone that would ring off the hook. I could see myself saying: 'Cheers & Tears Printing Company... How may I help you?' As though this was a call centre in the middle of some vast Hallmark-like organization."

Eventually, he garnered some press through the local paper about his greeting card business. "When the article came out, it listed our phone number, and people started calling in from all around the city to order greeting cards and stationery. To handle all the calls, we set up a separate phone line in my bedroom. Soon I was picking up my phone – just as I had imagined it two years earlier!"

A key lesson that his example provides us is one that he feels Dell Computers embodies and has been a key inspiration to him: "Dream big – and start small." Michael Dell started Dell Computer Corporation with less than $1000 and built that investment over time into a company with sales counted in the billions of dollars.

It wasn't too long after the greeting card success that Cameron would become known for his Internet-based businesses too. His first one launched when he was just 11; he sold his sister's Beanie Baby collection for $1000 on eBay. He paid her $100. She was happy and so was he! While he had stumbled onto a great business opportunity, there was a problem... his sister was all out of Beanie Babies. He had to start buying from the manufacturers. Since he could fill out the required application forms without talking to anyone on the phone, they didn't know he was barely 12. They didn't ask. Cameron didn't offer.

He was on a roll. Before his 13th birthday, he had become the second-largest Beanie Baby retailer on the Internet. "I was doing as much as $15,000 a month in sales," Cameron recalls, "outselling toy companies with as many as 15 or 20 employees. And it was completely a one-man business – unless you count the fact that I usually relied on my mom to drive me to the post-office to ship my orders."

That year he netted about $50,000 from Beanie Baby sales, and he wasn't even in high school yet. But he was having fun. He just chose to spend his after-school time differently than anyone else in his class. "I was doing okay in school – not great, but okay. In fact, everything about me was average, really. I was having a good time living the normal life of a normal teenager. It's just that I was throwing myself into my businesses in my spare time and not getting much sleep."

"Cameron was bright in many ways that school does not relate to," he recalls a teacher saying.

This could describe many people, maybe even you! Bob Proctor, for example, didn't quit high school (after attending for just three months)... he was asked to leave. Fraser Doherty of SuperJam left of his own will at the age of 16 to build his company. Some people like Rachel and the team at Suncayr do exceptionally well by continuing their formal education beyond high school and pursuing post-secondary degrees, but it's not for everyone. I'm quite certain the youth in this book would agree with me that lifelong learning is vitally important… but learning can take many forms. It doesn't always come from traditional sources.

In Cameron's book *You Call the Shots*, he mentions his B grade in an *Introduction to Business* course in the first semester of his only year of college. "How well you know something on an academic level has little to do with how well you will actually perform the task on your own later in life," he writes. "It's quite possible to ace a test and still not grasp its concepts. This is one of the fallacies of formal education."

Consider your education up until now. What have you learned and where? What has been the most useful? How do you learn most effectively? Are there opportunities in your life today through which you could pursue less conventional learning? As you move through the book and the lessons *it* offers, you will likely come up with some ideas about the skills and experience you'll need to pursue your goals and, in the long-term, build the life you'd love to live.

DESIGNING YOUR LIFE: 4 PRIMARY QUESTIONS

These are not likely the sorts of questions you're used to asking yourself, so know that the answers may arrive quickly, or more often, only after some committed soul searching – whatever that means to you. To consider them at the deepest possible level may take days or even weeks. And that's just fine.

#1 What do I love to do so much that I would pay people so that I could do it?

Virtually anything you love doing you can turn into a revenue source, if that's what you choose to do. Love playing with dogs? There are folks running very successful dog walking or canine daycare businesses. Maybe you are passionate about watching movies. How about becoming a film critic? The opportunities really are endless once you start looking and thinking.

"Your work is going to fill a large part of your life," said Steve Jobs in a now famous commencement speech at Stanford University. "The only way to be truly satisfied is to do what you believe is great work. And the only way to do great work is to love what you do."

Take Scott Young, for example. At 24, he decided he could do more with his passion for bartending than simply mixing drinks. And so Young went on to develop the now well-known theatrics and flair of extreme bartending, which popularized the notion that a bartender can also be an entertainer. This can include juggling bottles and mixers, or toying around with flammable liquors, or pouring three or more bottles at once, for example. Over the years, he has produced more than two dozen flair training videos that have sold in over 100 countries. His company has trained staff and performed demonstrations in 16 countries and has been the subject of hundreds of television interviews and print articles.

#2 *Describe your perfect work day.*

Early in my studies of the mind and human potential, I set the goal of becoming branch manager of a financial institution. At the time, I thought: wow, if I can really pull that off, my life would be made! What more could I possibly want? As it turned out… a lot.

> Follow your dreams: do what you really want to do. Don't start a business just because you hope to make money with it. And if you have to take a job for the money, get one that will allow you free time and energy to do what you love. Look for what's going to make you genuinely happy in life, and then do it. I have always placed fun, satisfaction, and fulfillment ahead of profit – and that has always ended up being very profitable.
> **Cameron Johnson, *You Call the Shots***

After being promoted to that dream position and working away at it for a couple of years, I realized it was not, in fact, where I wanted to be for the rest of my life. As a result, at 24, I passed up a promotion to head office. But that posed a major problem. I didn't know what I wanted to do. All I knew was that I wanted to leave banking. By now I was a firm believer in the power of visualization, of building and holding onto an image, but I felt stuck. I didn't know what the image was to build and hold!

....

> I love being my own boss. I never really realized that before, but I love being able to wake up in the morning and plan out my day the way I want it to be planned out, which is not something that you get to know until you start something like this.
>
> **Rachel Pautler, Suncayr CEO & Co-Founder**

....

The least I could do, I figured, was define the parameters of what I liked. So that's what I did. As it turned out, answering these questions was a huge help in enabling me to move at least in the direction I wanted to go, even if I wasn't clear on the final destination. So let's begin to define the characteristics of your perfect work day.

Consider the following questions. What would you prefer?

* Working predominantly on your own or with a group?
* To be self-employed or working for a larger company or organization?
* Working at home, in an office, in a coffee shop, or anywhere else?
* Working indoors or outdoors?
* To travel a lot or stay mostly in one place? Where?

Now, take the time to write out a paragraph describing your ideal work scenario. Once you've done that, you'll be in a much better position to recognize a great opportunity when it presents itself!

#3 If you knew it was impossible to fail, what is the number one thing you would do with your life?

This simplicity of this question is deceiving. But the answer, when you find it, is often enlightening. If you can remove the fear of failure from the picture, if you can eliminate all the barriers that hold you back… if you could dream in a vacuum… what would you do with your life? Let this be as crazy, ridiculous, out there, or seemingly unattainable as it needs to be. Remember, you don't yet have to concern yourself with the *how* of the dream. You simply need to use every creative tool at your disposal to figure out what it is. This is a great one.

#4 At 90, what memories would you like to cherish?

Imagine it's the day of your 90th birthday. You've just wrapped up a wonderful party, your friends and family have gone home, and you find yourself in your favourite rocking chair, quietly contemplating your life. In review, you see in your mind's eye all the wonderful things that have taken place. You feel a deep sense of gratitude. In this moment, consider what things would be absolutely unthinkable for you to have *not* tried.

I've often said that I would rather try something and fail, or at least have it not work out as planned, than to have not tried it at all and get stuck playing the *what if* game. *What if* I had started that business? *What if* I had the courage to accept that invitation or opportunity? *What if* _____ (fill in the blank)? Don't play that game. Be brave. Start it. Accept it. Try it. Every successful achiever I know will tell you that the learning experiences they gained from taking a leap of faith often proved invaluable for future, yet-to-be-dreamed-of tasks and accomplishments. Plus, there's no going back. Do the rocking chair test, and realize now what you'd like to cherish then.

DREAMS EXCEEDED: NICK & SWEETGRASS PRODUCTIONS

Time and time again, I've heard people who are living their dreams describe the experience as something they couldn't even imagine. Just when they thought it couldn't get any better, it did. I asked 20-something-year-old ski filmmaker, director, and producer Nick Waggoner how the reality of his life now compares to his original vision.

"Within the last couple of years, I've been very aware of my reality exceeding my dreams," he says. "And that's pretty cool; I'm so grateful for that. The other day I was up on Mt. Brennan looking out over all these incredible mountain peaks and it's just like, how did this happen? As a kid, this was more than I could have ever imagined or dreamed of."

Indeed. Chosen as one of *National Geographic's Adventurers of the Year* in 2012, Nick has on many levels travelled a great distance from a childhood home in New York City to his place in the world today, viewing the world through the lens of a camera. "It's been a way of going into these incredible places and bringing back stories and bringing back inspiration that can be shared with people who don't get to go there."

It almost didn't happen for him, though. He almost didn't make the leap. It was deciding, believing, and, in essence, beginning, which allowed all this to unfold. "I was studying economics and thinking that I should do something practical," he admits. "I was thinking I should ground my madness and creative ideas in something more rooted. But there was a definite point where I realized that wasn't very fun and fulfilling. So I took the other path. I went to my parents and told them I was going to take a semester off of school. I bought a video camera and flew down to South America and travelled through the mountains, through the jungle, and through the high peaks of the deserts. I had no idea what I was doing."

When Nick returned to college, it was clear that heading back to his economics classes wasn't an option. But there was a problem. All the film classes were full. Sometimes you *know* with every fibre of your being that you are making the right choice, and you simply cannot just accept the roadblocks and walk away. Nick knew. "I just walked in and I said I'm GOING to be in this class. I WILL be in this class. This class will not happen without me being in it."

The professor didn't see it that way. "I'm sorry, but the class is full," he insisted. That wasn't an option that Nick was willing to accept. He kept going. Every day. On the eighth day, the professor agreed to let him stay.

Fast forward nine years, and today Nick is collecting a growing list of awards for the projects and films that that he and his partners at Sweetgrass Productions have created; they accept (maybe even cherish) the immense work, risk, and sacrifice that's required to capture breathtaking mountain footage all over the world.

It was during a shoot in Japan that the idea of a night skiing project was born. While they had done some night shots in the past, Nick remembers looking at the big slopes they so often found themselves on, imagining them illuminated in just the right way. "What if we could shoot a big mountain *night* skiing film?" he thought. "How incredible would that be?" Yes, what if?

A few years later, when he thought the time was right, Nick approached one of their regular athletes, who agreed to work with him that particular winter on such a project. But after being on tour with their previous film, *Valhalla*, time was running out. The crew decided to push the project back a year.

Back in Japan, though, Nick had already planted the seed. Just a week after postponing the project, he was eating at a small, local hot spot, The Preserved Seed (yes, seriously). While waiting for his meal, he opened his phone to find an email from an agency for Phillips Ambilight TV, proposing that they make a big mountain *night* skiing film. "This has got to be a friend of mine who's playing a joke on me," thought Nick. "This can't be real." But it was very real. Less than three months later, they had a contract and were diving into filming this new project.

Wanting to do something and knowing *how* can be worlds apart. Nick had a clear vision of what he wanted to do, but he had no idea if it was actually possible to light up mountains of the size and scope they were imagining. In Alaska no less! "To go from months and months of researching lights and calling up manufacturers, to flying all the gear in and then being there in person witnessing all of it and seeing the slopes light up… all those moments make you realize that this is the most incredible job in the world. We're getting to realize our dreams left and right. It's incredible." It is incredible. And Nick is just getting started. **Where would you like your adventures to take you? Now is your time to decide.**

To get a sense of what they were facing, check out the behind-the-scenes video of this film, Afterglow. The crew had to manage thousands of pounds of lighting and video equipment and generators, in freezing temperatures, in the mountains, in the middle of winter. And the scenes are breathtaking.

YOUR LIST OF 100

In my youth program *Destiny by Design,* I often challenge participants to write down 100 goals during the course of one week. Yes, it seems like a lot… but here are three reasons why I encourage it as an exercise.

The sheer quantity will really push you to explore different areas of your life. If I asked you to write down only five, it may not be too much of a stretch for you… so you might not have to go too far outside what you're already experiencing. Although you can totally do this on your own, it can be helpful and a lot of fun to brainstorm with like-minded, positive people. You may hear about a goal they are pursuing that you'd like to emulate, or maybe it triggers a related idea that's tailor-made for you.

> Goals are just dreams taken seriously.
> **Cameron Johnson**

Once, while brainstorming in a group that included Mark Victor Hansen (co-author of the mega-best-selling *Chicken Soup for the Soul* series), I heard him mention that one of his many goals was to swim with dolphins. "What a fabulous idea," I thought, and added it to my list. Without hearing that, I may never have thought of it as a goal. Sure enough, barely a year later, I was windsurfing on the west coast of Australia and dolphins appeared not once but twice while I was swimming.

Would those encounters have happened if I had not written it down as a goal? Maybe. Maybe not. I can't guarantee that the dolphins got my memo. But you *will* be amazed that once you've created a set of heartfelt goals, you often just "happen" to be at the right place at the right time. Now that's cool. At first, it might scare you… but then it will never cease to amaze you.

Some goals are more important to you than others. While swimming with dolphins was an unforgettable experience, it wasn't on the top of my priority list. "This will be wonderful when it happens," I thought as I wrote it down. I have many goals like that. I'm confident they'll unfold for me, but they are not things I'm actively focusing on manifesting today. But regardless, recognizing these sorts of goals and adding them to your list brings some attention to them and, if nothing else, begins the positive process of attraction.

Gestation times will vary. Some of your goals may be short-term – their manifestation process might be measured in weeks or months; others might take years. When Andy-Stuart Hill was 21 years old, he sat at his kitchen table and wrote out a list of his lifetime goals. One of those goals – just one – was to visit 100 countries. I met him as a presenter at a Rotary Youth Leadership Camp, and I was impressed with his patience and persistence. At the age of 68, he visited Jordan – his 100th country! He celebrated with a personal, private ceremony and shared with me what he was thinking in that moment.

"It took 45 years to achieve this," he told himself. "There have been roadblocks, diversions, setbacks and frustrations, but you have remained true to your goal. You have earned the ultimate reward of enjoying beautiful sights and adventures in all these amazing countries, and meeting very interesting, wonderful people – the true object of my Goal-100."

Did he stop at 100? Of course not. Hill has now visited 132 countries on all seven continents – Antarctica was his last – and he's far from slowing down. "Joan, there are 196 countries!" he once reminded me.

SO HOW DO I COME UP WITH 100 GOALS?

Here is a very broad, general list that encompasses a variety of areas in your life. I encourage you to explore all these areas and any others you can think of. Mine all imaginable corners of your existence to come up with the most exciting, enlivening things you can have, do, or be.

Scan the list to get things rolling, and then (if you aren't already) sit somewhere quiet, comfortable, and safe, so you can close your eyes and lock into your imagination. Begin to dream.

Give yourself permission to really open up and contemplate what you would like to invite into your life. Again, no worrying about the how. Only consider the <u>what</u> at this point. And know that you can always go back and add to your master list. Here are some areas to consider:

Career & Business

* What position would you like at work? Can you create a new one?
* Would you like to change the industry you are working in?
* If you're self-employed, what would be your ideal your sales target?

Relationships

* Is there a friend or family member you would like to see more often?
* Do you want to increase your number of close friends?
* Do you want to find a new relationship or strengthen an existing one?

Personal Development
* What languages would you like to speak?
* What topics would you love to study?
* Would you like to attend seminars or trainings? On what? How often?

Financial
* How many sources of income would you like?
* What is your annual net income goal?
* What is your net worth goal?

Travel
* Where do want to visit, and what do you want to do?
* How often would you like to travel?
* Where would you like to stay? In ashrams? Resorts? Monasteries?
* Would you prefer backpacking or camping? Or exploring on a sailboat?

Health
* What is your perfect fitness level? Physical condition?
* What activities would you like to be physically able to do?

Everyday Life
* Where would you like to live? And in what sort of home?
* What sports would you learn? Play more of? Excel at?

There are heaps of information out there about goal setting and how to do it. I'm sharing with you what has worked for me. If this format doesn't resonate with you, find one that does. It's not the method of generating them but the pursuit of your goals that will help you discover all that you can be. Just decide what they are for you. That's the first step.

Q: CAN A GOAL BE <u>TOO BIG</u>?

A: NO! Absolutely not.

Around 1977, Bill Gates and his co-founder at Microsoft shared their vision of seeing a computer on every desk and in every home, running Microsoft software. That was a *huge* idea at the time. Gates has since pointed out that a lot of very smart people at the time just didn't get it. "Why would somebody need a computer?" they'd ask.
"It's kind of a silly idea!" Yes… that's what they really said. Today, it's hard to imagine not having one in your pocket, let alone on your desk!

If, in your mind's eye, you can see yourself already in possession of your goal, I believe that's proof enough that you can accomplish it. Will you know how? In most cases, absolutely not! Consider the real reason for a goal. *The purpose of having goals is not to get stuff. Ultimately, the purpose is to grow.* Pursuing goals makes you dig deep and discover the resources of talent and ability you have within you, just waiting to be expressed.

CAPTAIN YOUR OWN SHIP

Earl Nightingale is widely considered to be the father of personal development. He shared with the world so many wonderful metaphors and analogies. Here's one of my favourites; it has stuck with me since I first heard it at 19:

"People with goals succeed because they know where they are going. It's that simple. Think of a ship leaving a harbour. And think of it with a complete voyage mapped out and planned. The captain and crew know exactly where *it's going and how long it will take. It has a definite goal. 9,999 times out of 10,000 it will get to where it started out to get.*

"Now let's take another ship, just like the first. Only let's not put a crew on it or a captain at the helm. Let's give it no aiming point, no goal, no destination. We just start the engines and let it go. I think you'll agree with me that if it gets out of the harbour at all, it'll either sink or wind up on some deserted beach a derelict. It can't go anyplace because it has no destination and no guidance. It's the same with a human being."

It's been my experience that a person with goals that are in alignment with their values will accomplish more in a few short years than most people do in a lifetime. Why? Because they know where they are going. They know that they are the captain, and they choose a destination. With that clarity, decision-making becomes easier. When we know where we're headed, we can then take advantage of our inner compass… the one that tells us if a particular decision or activity is on course or if it's instead leading us away from our ultimate destination.

People who seem to accomplish so much in their lives have exactly the same amount of hours in a day as everyone else. The biggest difference between them and anyone else is simply that they have set decisive goals. When they get out of bed in the morning, they know what it is that they are working toward.

CHAPTER THREE

DECISION TIME

Your next job is to review your list and pick out those goals that you are prepared to actively pursue today. Is there a perfect number? Not that I've discovered. I suggest that you focus on a few areas in your life where you are ready to commit to making some real headway. And remember that over time, our priorities shift. Our values change. But you need to start somewhere, so start where you're at. Which items on your list seem most relevant TODAY? Of all the things you came up with, which are the ones that you are prepared to take action on? These are the ones that you will be giving more energy to right now. They are the seeds you'll soon be planting in the rich and fertile soil of your mind.

Note that the key words here are *commit* and *action*. To accomplish your goals, recognize that you'll have to start doing some things differently. If you simply continue doing what you've always done, you'll continue to get what you've always gotten. Seems obvious when you think about it, right?

But herein lies a problem. *You already know of steps you could be taking* to improve the quality of your life, or to move in the direction of accomplishing some of what you wrote down, but the problem is that you're not doing them. Furthermore, and the bit that's more of a challenge, is that you don't know *why* you're not doing them. Sure, you might be able to come up with some surface reasons and excuses, but if you're truly honest with yourself and plow past your fears – whatever they are – you're probably shaking your head. "Why the heck *aren't* I already doing what I know I can do to improve my results?" you might be asking.

It's simple. But not necessarily an easy fix. It's because you and I don't act from our conscious thoughts but rather through the filter of the paradigm that is rooted deeply in our subconscious. Here's how Bob Proctor defines paradigms:

"Paradigms are a multitude of habits that guide every move you make. They affect the way you eat, the way you walk, even the way you talk. They govern your communication, your work habits, your successes and your failures. For the most part, your paradigms didn't originate with you. They're the accumulated inheritance of other people's habits, opinions, and belief systems. Yet they remain the guiding force in YOUR life."

Your paradigm acts as the filter through which you view the world. You can think of it as your unique internal operating system. Because it resides in your subconscious, it is largely applied without your awareness.

Maybe you are someone who has difficulty meeting new people. That was always the case for me. On a conscious, rational level, I knew how wonderful it would be if I were more outgoing; I could imagine the interesting people I'd meet, the opportunities that might present themselves, what I would learn… and yet continued to keep to myself. Why? Because it wasn't my thoughts that were controlling my behaviour. It was (and is) my paradigm. This is why, on a conscious level, we can *know* what it is we want to do or need to do and yet still fail to act.

Perhaps someone else is stuck dreaming of a sport they would like to try. It looks like a ton of fun, and it would be great to do it with their friends; they'd love to jump in right away and try it. They don't, though, because they're afraid of how they'll look it they don't do it perfectly off the bat. Even though on a conscious level, they are eager to participate (and they may even actively realize that everyone begins as a beginner), their paradigm blocks them.

Fear is negative goal setting.

In the next section, I'll show you how to recognize and change those aspects of your paradigm that need changing so you can do the things you want to do with your life. Think of it as your OS upgrade! I'll help you choose the right program and even show you how to do the install. This shift is vital, as we cannot experience permanent change in our lives until our paradigm has been adjusted accordingly. It's this process that I used to become comfortable not only meeting new people but speaking in front of large audiences too. I attribute it to every major trait adjustment and major accomplishment in my life. And it starts with the goals you picked to pursue RIGHT NOW.

BRINGING YOUR GOALS TO LIFE

It's not enough to create a list of your goals and then toss them in a drawer or close the electronic file. Rather, you want to live, eat, and breathe like you already have that which you desire. If you can hold it in your head, eventually you will hold it in your hand. "If you have the desire," Deepak Chopra has said, "you have the means to create it. In the desire itself is the means of creation." But do remember that there is always a gestation period. Remember the orange seed? You don't plant the seed and expect the fruit the next day. The seed needs to be nurtured. It needs warmth and water. It needs to be planted in a fertile environment that's conducive to healthy growth. And it needs time to germinate. Long before the first seed leaves break through the soil, the soon-to-be tree is busy bursting out of its shell and becoming what it will become – even though that underground part of the process is invisible to you. The more we study human potential, the more we fine-tune our understanding of the creative process and learn to trust that we can set in motion things that we cannot see.

I love the way Geneviève Behrend explains this in her classic work *Your Invisible Power*, which she penned after studying with Judge Thomas T. Troward in England. Troward studied religious science and was best known for his Edinburgh and Dore Lectures on Mental Science, published in the early 1900s. Having gone through these works, I can assure you… they are not what I would call easy reading.

Enter Geneviève Behrend. The year was 1912. Though Behrend had a desire to study with Troward, there were a number of challenges, to say the least. Firstly, he had never accepted a student and wasn't interested in having one. Secondly, he lived in England, and she lived in New York; it would cost her the enormous sum of $20,000 (which she did not have) to travel to him by ship. Fortunately, she had already studied the mind and human potential enough to understand, even then, that she could not let present circumstances determine her fate. She knew it was essential that she build and hold the image of her goal. Every morning and every evening, Behrend visualized counting out 20 one thousand dollar bills, buying her ticket to London, travelling on the ship and being accepted as Troward's pupil. Six weeks later, the money appeared in her life.

Behrend bought her ticket, boarded the ship, and eventually ended up in England. At first glance, Troward refused her. But thanks to incredible persistence, Behrend eventually became the first – and only – personal student of the judge.

"The exercise of the visualizing faculty keeps your mind in order, and attracts to you the things you need to make life more enjoyable in an orderly way," she later wrote. *"If you train yourself in the practice of deliberately picturing your desire and carefully examining your picture, you will soon find that your thoughts and desires proceed in a more orderly procession than ever before. Having reached a state of ordered mentality you are no longer in a constant state of mental hurry. Hurry is fear and consequently destructive.*

"In other words, when your understanding grasps the power to visualize your heart's desire and hold it with your will, it attracts to you all things requisite to the fulfillment of that picture by the harmonious vibrations of the law of attraction [...] Everyone visualizes, whether they know it or not. Visualizing is the great secret of success. The conscious use of this great power attracts to you multiplied resources, intensifies your wisdom, and enables you to make use of advantages which you formerly failed to recognize."

Build the image. Hold it with your will. Get on with the work. We are creatures of habit. And if we are going to chart a new course and do things differently, the first step is in the building. But the holding with will is key. If we don't, we go back to what we are comfortable with… the way things were.

THE POWER OF THE VISION BOARD

One of the most powerful tools I have come across to help me keep the images I am working toward front and centre has come to be known more recently as a **vision board**. It's a collection of images you find or create and display on a board that hangs prominently in your home; put it somewhere where you'll see it often.

As a whole, a vision board represents your ideal future. You can use anything that to you represents, symbolizes, or illustrates your primary goals. Consider including inspirational words or quotes that speak to you or offer the support you need, as well as descriptions of personal traits or characteristics you'd like to build on or improve. Overall, keep it simple and clear. If you have a board that's too cluttered, it can be distracting and difficult to focus on each important area.

There was a time in my life during which I wanted to sell a business. The business had a respectable amount of goodwill in our community, and that goodwill was built into my asking price. The real estate agent I was planning to list with insisted that the local market, at that time, was not interested in paying for goodwill. I disagreed. I could tell he was focused on finding a buyer only from the surrounding area. My partner and I had reason to believe that the business would be attractive to a number of people throughout the Pacific Rim. We decided to stick with our instincts and market it ourselves. The very first thing I did was go to an office supply store and buy an *Agreement of Purchase & Sale* – not to have it ready once a buyer came along but rather to complete it right away for the exact sale price and terms we wanted. I then taped it to the wall next to my bed, where I could see it every day. Guess what? We sold the business the way we wanted and got what we wanted.

Later, when it came time to sell a house, we had a similar conversation with yet another realtor. This time he felt our price was too high... nothing had sold in our area for as much as we were asking. Using the exact same steps, we sold the house privately for the return we felt it warranted.

Why? It wasn't just the piece of paper I taped to my bedroom wall. You and I are not going to reach our goals simply by creating our vision boards and looking at them every day. They are, however, excellent reminders for us to pause and visualize the good that we desire. When we can see ourselves on the screen of our mind having, doing, or being our goal like it's already been achieved, we move into a different vibration – one that is in harmony with that which we desire; this sets up an attractive force between us and our goal. No, this does not cause a bag of money to fall in our lap or drop the car of our dreams in the driveway. **The Law of Attraction** doesn't bring you the goal. But what you *will* receive are inspirations and insights. If you are listening for them, trust in them, and take action accordingly, you'll find that you often end up in the right place at the right time. Just like with the dolphins. But you must take action. If you do, you'll just happen to meet the right person or notice the right opportunity. People who don't understand this process will say you were lucky. But it's not luck. It's law. **Universal Law.** And universal law rocks. Big time.

One of my favourite examples of someone creating a visual representation of her goals is Philippine-born Charmaine Pempengco, an incredible singer better known as Charice. Raised by her single mom, Charice began entering singing contests at the age of seven to help support her family. But even before that, as early as the age of three, she was drawing pictures of her dreams in what she called her *dream notebook*;

notably, they included sketches of Canadian superstar Celine Dion and even scenes of her and Celine singing together!

> All you have to do is think and it will be. You're attracting other people to help realize that goal. And it's really just about closing your eyes and taking a deep breath and – to really oversimplify this – saying: 'I'm going to do this. I'm going to get this done, and I'm going to make this movie (or whatever it is).' And that confidence will attract all of the tools and all of the support and resources you need to achieve that goal.
> **Nick Waggoner, Sweetgrass Productions**

Thanks to much determination, years of hard work, and of course her exceptional talent, Charice became an online YouTube sensation, and many doors began to open for her. In 2008, Oprah Winfrey invited the then 16-year-old to be a guest on an episode dubbed *Dreams Come True*, where Charice sang an incredibly moving version of Celine's *My Heart Will Go On*, accompanied on piano by David Foster. But the very best part, of course, was when Oprah surprised Charice by inviting Celine to appear via satellite. The young singer burst into tears of excitement and gratitude. To top it off, Celine invited Charice to sing a duet with her later that year at New York City's Madison Square Garden to a sold-out crowd. She accepted, and it was an amazing performance.

Watching Charice realizing her dream – one she had drawn and visualized for so many years – reminded me of hockey great Wayne Gretzky. In his autobiography, Gretzky expresses how it felt skating around the rink, carrying the coveted Cup above his head after winning the Stanley Cup final. "I must have rehearsed how I would do it ten thousand times," he recalls, "and when it finally came true… it was like an electric jolt up my spine."

"The Door was the door in our locker room that led to the tunnel," he recalls in *Gretzky: An Autobiography*. "We taped a lot of famous pictures to that door. Bobby Orr, Potvin, Beliveau, all holding the Cup. We'd stand and look at it and envision ourselves doing it. I really believe if you visualize yourself doing something, you can make that image come true. Sometimes I'd catch Cof practically staring a hole in that door. If they'd let us unhinge that door and bring it to the bench, we probably would have."

Seeing glimpses of your positive future every day helps keep your mind focused on the direction you want to go. Ideally, you'll want to see your board just before going to bed and when you first wake up, so a great place to have it is in your bedroom. It's certainly a lovely view to be greeted by as you roll out of bed – it's a great way to start the day. I take time every morning to scan what's on the board while I'm still quiet and relaxed and before my day really gets rolling. I see in my mind's eye that I'm already in possession of the goals on my board and really explore what it feels like to have already accomplished them.

It's worth remembering that this is how you put yourself in the vibratory rate that matches the good that you desire. You're remembering the seed you planted and providing it great nourishment every time you connect with it so deeply.

I encourage you to do the same thing before going to bed at night.

You may be heading off to sleep, but your subconscious is not. It's the perfect imagery to hold as you drift off. Sleep is an amazing problem solving tool at your disposal! Once you start doing this, you will be delighted at the inspirations you'll receive during the night and even the next morning. Have a journal or a pad of paper near your bed to record ideas the moment you're conscious. It's amazing how quickly they disappear once you're fully awake.

I was reminded of the importance of focusing on where we want to go (as opposed to where we currently are) when I took a motorcycle course a few years back in preparation for earning my motorcycle licence. The instructor was demonstrating how to make a very sharp hairpin turn at slow speed. She made it look so easy. When any of us tried to duplicate what we saw her just do... well, suffice it to say, it wasn't pretty. None of us could follow in her tracks. Until she told us her secret, that is. Focus on where you want to go, she suggested, and not where you are. As long as I was looking just in front of me, I could *not* get the bike to turn. It was only after I literally focused on my destination by looking hard left, or hard right, that the bike would follow.

Life is like that. If we base our goal setting on our present circumstances, we'll just create more of the same. I hope I've been able to demonstrate that to you. When you begin to tap into your unlimited potential by utilizing your higher faculties – by imagining where you want to go – you open yourself up to amazing possibilities.

SHARING (OR NOT) YOUR GOALS

Evidence of whether or not you can achieve a goal is *not* found in your past results, as you might expect, but rather in your present vision. In other words, how strongly are you holding that goal-oriented image? If you can see it and feel it in every fibre of your being, that's all the proof you need. But that may not be proof enough for other people to buy into your dreams. So how do you handle that? Simple. Don't tell them.

If you have positive, supportive, loving companions, sure – share with them, if you feel it's appropriate. But it's not necessary. And definitely avoid sharing your aspirations with those who may respond negatively. You don't need that!

Back in my banking days, I mustered up the courage to tell a colleague about my hope of becoming a bank manager. Immediately, he pointed out how young I was and how such a thing wasn't possible. It had never been done at my age, he reminded me, and so on and so forth. Despite his minimizing of my potential, he did teach me something valuable that day: unless I was craving negative feedback, he wasn't the person with whom I should discuss my big, seemingly impossible dreams. We continued to work together for a number of years, and I loved his sense of humour and his way of interacting with the staff. Any conversation with him about my goals, though, was off the table. I am so thankful that by then I had already begun studying this material, so I understood that even though he was my senior in both age and company position, he was expressing only his opinion – not an accurate reflection of my actual potential.

Eventually, I was recruited by and accepted a job promotion with another financial institution. Once I'd been working there for a few months, I learned that my new company was looking to hire a manager for one of its branches. It was then I knew for sure I had made the right move. That very day, after my shift, I drove to the branch in question so I could see it in person and hold an image of what my soon-to-be branch and personal office would look like. Shortly thereafter, I was fortunate to have a telephone conversation with the president of the company. Since I had recently come from another financial institution, he wanted to know if there was anyone I knew from my previous employer that we could lure away. In short, he asked, did I know of anyone for the position? "Other than myself, no," I told him. He laughed.

I suppose I shouldn't have been surprised. I was 22 years old at the time, and he didn't know me very well. "You'll get there," he assured me. "It just might not be for a couple of years." It turned out to be mere months. The company couldn't immediately find anyone they felt was suitable, so they asked if I would accept the role of *acting* manager until they found someone permanently for the position. A number of weeks later, I no longer had to act. The job was mine.

If I had not been diligently studying the mind and human potential, I would have likely a) not set a goal in the first place, b) not set *that* goal, and therefore, c) when asked if I knew of anyone for the branch manager position, might have had nothing to say. I learned quite strongly from that experience that no one could have guessed at my potential, and my primary responsibility was to act as though I was already in possession of my goal. I knew I needed to hold that image strongly, regardless of what others said and regardless of outside circumstances. "People are always blaming their circumstances for what they are," wrote George Bernard Shaw in *Mrs. Warren's Profession*. "I don't believe in circumstances. The people who get on in this world are the people who get up and look for the circumstances they want, and if they can't find them, make them."

Recognize too, that there are a lot of dream-thieves out there in the world. Many of them even have good intentions. They love you and don't want to see you disappointed or hurt; they are scared to see you fail. They may not understand that a failure is in fact an incredibly valuable learning experience, a chance to figure out what *doesn't* work. In many respects, they'd like to see you play it safe. And still others would feel threatened by your success. In their eyes, *your* success makes *them* look less successful. You'll need to be prepared for this. Don't be phased by it. **Remember... Build the image. Hold it with your will. Get on with the work.**

DEEP & A LIFESAVING IDEA

Deep Shankar Saha set a goal – to solve the blood shortage problem in his country of India. Despite a population of more than 1.2 billion people, India faces a blood shortage of three million units. Deep discovered that people were willing to donate, but the real issue was what could happen to the blood after the donation was made. Since blood has a shelf life, there is the issue of expiry. A bigger, more challenging roadblock, though, is the potential for blood smuggling, or it being sold to the highest bidder. It means that sometimes, if you need blood, you can't get it.

In 167 countries throughout the world, there exists an amazing network of more than 8,000 Rotaract Clubs, whose members range from 18-30 years old; they meet twice a month to exchange ideas, plan activities and projects, and socialize. Deep is the president of his local club in Kolkata, India: the Rotaract Club of Altruism. He knew what a resourceful, creative, positive group of people the members of the Rotaract Club were. He had some new ideas about how to approach the blood shortage issue, and not surprisingly, his team was on board. They liked the concept and planned to adopt it as part of the club's project. "We made plans to implement it immediately," says Deep, "as it was the need of the hour." And a great need it was!

Earlier in the year, their club had organized a blood donation camp in an attempt to address this problem. It went exceedingly well. They spent 15,000 rupees (about $250) and received blood donations from 49 people. Each donor was given a blood card, which meant that when *that* person was in need of blood in the future, they would be given priority and be able to access the blood they required at 1/10th of the cost. At least, that was the way it was supposed to work. "After a few months, one of the donors needed blood for his relative," Deep explains. "We approached the blood bank, informed them of the need, and showed them the card. Instead of coming to our rescue, they said that their blood banks were dry, and it would not be possible for them to help us. The reason was evident. They were making a business with the donated blood. Giving us blood with a low price would result in a loss." Clearly, having more blood donation camps was not the answer.

But maybe a *virtual* blood bank, thought Deep, would do the trick. It eliminates the spoilage problem and also stops the illegal siphoning of blood for commercial use. It's brilliant in its simplicity. The virtual blood bank (VBB) is an online database that stores details of the potential donor's essential information – things like blood type and contact information – which are accessed when an emergency arises. This data is sorted according to geographic location, so help is available on short notice. The Club maintains a 24/7 phone helpline that individuals in need or the hospital can call when blood is needed. The patient's requirements are matched up with a registered donor, and the physical blood donation can take place.

"In November 2014," Deep recalls, "a lady called me up to say that a newborn baby needed blood platelets immediately for a blood transfusion. He was in a critical condition. Within 45 minutes, we were able to arrange a donor and save the life of the baby."

Recently, a man came to India from Bangladesh for his wife's chemotherapy treatment at Tata Medical Center, Kolkata. Her need for blood, though, was greater than Deep and his team had access to. Rather than turn the couple away, the Rotaract Club of Altruism sprang into action and arranged a replacement blood donation camp right in the Tata Medical Center! The man's wife recovered from blood cancer and was, at the time of this writing, alive and well in Bangladesh.

Registration to the virtual blood bank is growing, but Deep dreams of seeing it expand across India and abroad. "The more we grow," he points out, "the faster we will be able to overcome the growing problems related to blood shortages."

At the moment, the growth is entirely in their hands. Deep and the other members of the Rotaract Club of Altruism – which in 2014 was named *Best New Club* at the District Rotaract Conference – run the VBB as volunteers and regularly encourage others to get involved. It's working. It's saving lives. And it started… like so many wonderful, successful ideas, as a single thought: how can I make this better?

How can you improve your life? The lives of those around you? How can you have, do, or be, anything that you'd like, and, in doing so, make the world a better place? First, you have to commit to the decision.

SO HAVE YOU DECIDED? ARE YOU IN?

Have you made the decision to pursue your goals? You will know for sure when you look at your actions. Too often people confuse talking about their goals with taking action. Or they'll plan and plan and plan but never act. That's not deciding.

Deciding is making a commitment to yourself that you will do something and then DOING IT. This is a key component to *the way success works*. You can decide to pursue a goal before figuring out how it will all come together. Remember, the purpose of a goal is for you to grow. So if it's a big enough dream you want to chase, there is no way you'll know how to reach it when you start out. If you make the commitment to proceed, though, I bet you'll know – at the very least – how you need to begin. Go as far as you can see. When you get there, you'll see how to go further.

ACT TWO

BELIEVE

CHAPTER FOUR

THE STATE OF MIND... IT MUST BE BELIEF

Anything the mind can conceive and believe, it can achieve.
Napoleon Hill

Napoleon Hill is best known for his classic work, *Think & Grow Rich*, published in 1937. The book presents a formula for success derived from Hill's studying and interviewing hundreds of the most rich and successful people in America over a 20 year period, including Andrew Carnegie, Henry Ford, Theodore Roosevelt, Charles Schwab, John D. Rockefeller, Thomas A. Edison, Woodrow Wilson, Dr. Alexander Graham Bell and Wilbur Wright.

Over those years, it became so very clear to him that *anything* the mind can conceive and believe it can achieve. Anything! Not what's within reason or even what's *realistic*. At the time when Wilbur Wright and his brother Orville were building and selling bicycles, they dreamed of a world where people could fly through the air in a pilot-controlled flying machine (now known as... an airplane). At the time, that was a crazy idea. They faced much scepticism and ridicule, to say the least; fortunately, they didn't allow the naysayers to knock them off course.

In the first section, I suggested that you find a spot to enjoy a calm, relaxed state of being without disruption, where you could turn inward and begin to explore what you would truly like to have, do, or be. You were drawing on your imagination to conceive, or dream up, some ideas about the future you'd like to create. Now is the time to check in on your beliefs. Deep down, do you *believe* you can manifest your heart's desire?

That genuine belief is a critical component of success. "There is a difference between WISHING for a thing and being READY to receive it," wrote Hill. "No one is ready for a thing, until he believes he can acquire it. The state of mind must be BELIEF, not mere hope or wish." A belief is no more or less than your personal evaluation of something – anything. And the most interesting and empowering realization about beliefs is that you are free, at any time, to re-evaluate your beliefs about anything!

Imagine that you are a juror in a court room. A door opens, and the defendant is escorted in. He is, by far, the meanest looking dude you've ever seen; he's downright scary. The charges against him are read. Do you think it's possible – having not yet heard any of the evidence for or against him – that you have already begun to shape your belief about this man? That you already believe him to be guilty? Of course it's possible. And it probably happens far too often.

But you stay in the courtroom and hear the trial. You might be there all day or several days or even many weeks. Eventually, when the jurors find themselves in deliberation behind closed doors, you might have come to the conclusion that this man is innocent. And other jurors may agree. So how did you change your mind? It's quite simple, really; the shift in beliefs came about by gathering information and re-evaluating it.

So step back and consider what that means in the context of other beliefs you hold. When you gather information about yourself, for example, and re-evaluate it with a critical eye, the beliefs you carry around about you as a human and what you are capable of doing can – and will – change. But an open mind is absolutely essential.

There are likely a number of beliefs that you carry about yourself that are both healthy and helpful – maybe you're resourceful, persistent, or have a great sense of humour, for example. These may have helped you achieve the successes that you've enjoyed in your life until now. If there are things that you've wanted to accomplish in your life, however, that you have not yet acted upon, you are surely carrying some limiting beliefs too: beliefs that are holding you back. These limiting beliefs are part of your paradigm that I mentioned earlier. They are preventing you from seeing and acting with your true capacity.

When you get the feeling that you can't do something you'd really love to do, understand that the feeling is not actually a reflection of your potential. Rather, it's a reflection of your paradigm.

FROM LOCAL TO GLOBAL: FRASER'S SUPERJAM

Many of us have a part-time job after school when we are young. Some of us have a few! From my first paper route (delivering newspapers before sunrise in every kind of Canadian weather), to mopping floors at a bakery, to working behind the counter at a dry-cleaning shop (maybe a few years before I was supposed to), I always loved the idea of having money in my pocket. To me, it meant independence. The way I figured it, since I earned it, I could spend it as I pleased. Maybe my parents had a different opinion, but *I* felt good about that conclusion anyway.

I didn't recognize it at the time, but looking back, I realize that I've learned something from just about everywhere I worked – even in those earlier days. Sometimes I was learning what *not* to do, but regardless, I was frequently picking up skills that I would draw upon in the future.

For some young people, those early days evolve into their life's work. At 13, Fraser Doherty picked up a job in his hometown of Edinburgh, Scotland, selling bacon and sausages door-to-door for a local entrepreneur. He quickly realized that he enjoyed the relationships he was building with his growing customer base, and he did quite well. This was the first time he had really known an entrepreneur – his boss – and he liked what he saw. "I found his way of life fascinating," says Fraser. "Seeing him growing his business and being in control of his lifestyle made me more and more certain that I wanted to start up a business of my own one day."

As it turns out, that day would come within the year when he paid a visit to his grandmother, who was famous among family and friends for her spectacular homemade jam. It was then that Fraser, one of her biggest fans, had an epiphany. Toast in one hand and a mason jar in the other, he realized that his business would be jam. And not just any jam, but his gran's well-loved secret recipe.

He was so excited by the idea that he immediately convinced his grandmother to teach him everything he needed to know about crafting his first batch. With an investment of two British pounds ($3) for a few oranges and a bag of sugar, he produced his first few jars of marmalade. Before they were completely cooled, Fraser was out the door with his plastic bucket full of product, going door-to-door. He came home that day having doubled his money. "I felt like I had accomplished something huge," he says. "I had created a profit completely on my own with nothing more than a few oranges and some sugar."

Over time, his variety of jams grew – as did his client base. So much so, in fact, that by the age of 16, Fraser left school to turn his growing business into a full-time career. His parents, fortunately, were very supportive. "I was lucky to have parents who told me that the most important thing in life is to find something that you love," he admits. "If you can get up in the morning and look forward to your work, then that's success. In my case, I figured out early on that making jam was what I wanted to do."

It didn't take long for him to outgrow the confines of the family kitchen. Soon he was processing over 1,000 jars of jam every week, selling them at markets and to small shops all over Scotland. When his parents could barely sneak in to cook dinner, Fraser realized he needed a new plan. If the business was going to grow any further, he'd have to come up with a big idea to make the leap to factory production.

At the time, the jam business wasn't trendy. It fact, it was in decline. As a product, jam had an old-fashioned image and, thanks to its high sugar content, was thought to be tremendously unhealthy. Fraser decided he was going to shift that whole notion by reinventing the wheel. Or rather, the product. After copious research, dozens of trial batches, and many failed concepts, he achieved success: a jam made solely from fruit and juice. "It tasted beautiful, really fruity and natural, the way jam is supposed to be." His big idea, SuperJam, was born.

The next challenge was getting SuperJam into pantries across Scotland. It's one thing to create a fabulous product and quite another to help people discover it. But a newspaper ad provided just that opportunity. Waitrose, the much-loved British supermarket chain, was planning to open a store right in Edinburgh, and their ad encouraged local food producers to come out to a one-day event where they could pitch their ideas to the supermarket's most senior buyers. (It bears mentioning that

Waitrose is a big deal. It's a chain of British supermarkets that forms the food retail division of Britain's largest employee-owned retailer, the John Lewis Partnership. Not only do they sell to the general population of the UK, but the company has a royal warrant to supply groceries, wine, and spirits to Queen Elizabeth II and Prince Charles too!)

The day arrived, and Fraser stood in line with all the other hopefuls for his chance to make his pitch. Soon enough, he found himself sitting in front of the senior jam buyer. While the buyer found it refreshing to see a teenager come along with such a grandiose dream, he pointed out that Fraser had a long way to go until his product could hit the shelves of a leading supermarket like Waitrose. The buyer did promise, though, that if Fraser came back in a year's time having accomplished three things, he'd consider launching the product. Here they are:

1. Line up a proper factory to produce the quantity and quality necessary and at a competitive price,
2. Create a good-looking brand that people would love, and
3. Come up with a better recipe.

Each of the list items was a huge task, none of which Fraser knew how he would make happen. But nonetheless, he was encouraged; at least he wasn't flat out rejected! He didn't, however, have the money to pay an agency for the branding work, nor did have the money to build a factory.

Too often, lack of money stops people from pursuing their dreams. They tell themselves that they love to do something, but *can't* because they don't have the funds to support it. And while perhaps the funds aren't available in that moment, paying for something with money isn't the only option! You can trade, barter, provide other services... the solutions are often only limited by our thinking.

I once saw a very creative ad to address the high cost of housing. A young man who was a builder found that it was difficult to save enough to cover a down payment for a house of his own while paying rent every month. His solution was clever. He put out an offer to build a cabin, for free, for anyone in the area with a suitable parcel of land. The land-owner would provide the materials, and he would use his knowledge, experience, skills, and tools to craft the structure for them. In lieu of payment for his services, he would live in the cabin he built, rent-free, for two years so that he could continue to work and save money for a down payment for his own property.

While I recognize that there are many people for whom this arrangement would not work, I saw it as a reminder that often the only deficit is in our creative thinking. If we make the decision to forge ahead and are willing to open up to other possibilities, it's amazing what problems we can solve and the unique situations we can find ourselves in.

Fraser rejected the branding quotes he received from various design agencies, one that was for nearly $50,000. Instead, he was able to convince a local advertising agency to buy into his vision when they agreed to work on the project for free in exchange for future work.

Money also presented a problem when it came to sourcing a factory. Since Fraser didn't have that sort of cash in hand or, as a teenager, the ability to approach a bank for financing, he had to find a factory willing to put up the working capital to buy fruit, jars, and labels to make the first batch of tens of thousands of jars, a risk of roughly $75,000 at the time. He travelled all over the country, from the tiny islands off the north coast of Scotland to the big cities of England, trying to find someone to produce SuperJam. They all said no… except one. But that's all Fraser needed.

So one year after first meeting the Waitrose buyer, Fraser was ready to again make his pitch, and he did. This time, the buyer told Fraser that the factory wasn't suitable, his labelling was off the mark, and he didn't like the new flavours. SuperJam was rejected again. "Am I just wasting my time?" Fraser recalls thinking.

But the teen was determined to march onward. After getting some good marketing advice, Fraser came up with a new branding concept for his dream product. He found a suitable factory that would front the costs of producing the first batch, and together they created new jam flavours that were the best ever. It worked. In March 2007, SuperJam arrived on Waitrose store shelves.

"After I had spent a couple of years working on trying to get my products into the supermarket, it was a very special moment when, at 18, my dream was realized. I was able to visit a local store and see my jars lined up on the shelf," says Fraser. "It was the moment where everything I had focused on came true." Today, SuperJam sells in a dozen countries across the globe, on the shelves of over 2,000 individual stores.

One of the creative ways that Fraser got his product into hundreds of independent shops was by encouraging SuperJam fans to tell them, via their website, about a shop in their area where they thought the jam should be sold. That allowed Fraser and his team to send out a postcard to the suggested shop, letting them know that one of their customers believed they should stock SuperJam, with some information about the products and an introductory offer for the store. If the outlet placed an order, they would send out a free jar of jam to the person who made the suggestion. Fraser tells me they'll soon be launching a competition to encourage people to help them find great new outlets *around the world*. Simple. And brilliant.

What made Fraser think he could make a go of his jam business? What allowed him to see the opportunity in the first place? Let's take a closer look at why we believe the things we do.

When you were born, the faculties of your conscious mind – the parts that give you the ability to accept or reject ideas – were not yet fully developed. I can share an idea with you now, and as an adult you have the capacity to agree with it or reject it. When you arrived on the scene as an infant, however, that reasoning ability was not yet fully formed.

That means that as young children, you and I were open channels to the ideas presented to us. We knew of no option other than to accept those ideas, uncritically, no matter where they came from – be it parents, grandparents, brothers, sisters, or anyone else in our close circle. We were given ideas about what was right and wrong, what was good and bad, and, of course, you were given ideas about yourself.

All of these ideas come together to form the basis of your paradigm. That paradigm, of course, includes your self-image. The image you have of yourself is based on your conditioning and includes past experiences, and it causes you to view the world in a certain way. *It determines your belief about what you are able to accomplish.* Logically, then, your self-image strongly impacts your goal setting and the scope and beauty of the vision you can dream up of your future self. This is why it's *so* important to release the restrictions imposed by your existing paradigm as much as possible when you start considering what you would truly like to have, do, or be.

THE GRAND DEBATE: NATURE & NURTURE

In 1994, I watched a documentary on the making of the movie *American Me*, a film centred around gang life in East Los Angeles that starred and was directed and produced by Edward James Olmos. The filming took place on the cusp of three gang territories. "There was no way we could film here without the cooperation of the rival gangs," Olmos explained in the documentary *Lives in Hazard*. The film crew was justifiably concerned about drive-by shootings, which, at the time, were happening on a near daily basis. "After weeks of negotiation," says Olmos, "they agreed to a truce, and many of them became actors in the movie."

One scene in the documentary really stood out for me. It described how one morning, when the film crew arrived on location, they encountered a three-year-old boy, all alone, on a tricycle. After picking him up and talking with him, Olmos managed to get a good laugh out of the boy. "For whatever reason, his parents were not around," he recalls. "He was a very tough little boy who had been on the street for a very long time… and seeing that makes you sensitive to the fact that *environment is everything*. He was the future gang member."

Know that this observation was not based on some inherent lack of potential. Just like you, that little boy has an inner Golden Buddha. But throughout his whole short life, negative influences and experiences have layered one on top of the other to shroud its brilliance and hide his true capacity to achieve anything he desires. Instead, even at just three years old, he already has a toughness about him.

Contrast the experiences of this boy with the ideas and experiences to which Siobhan Mullen was exposed in *her* childhood. "I grew up in a family with parents who were very much feminists," says Siobhan, who became president of an aerospace company at the age of 33. "Most importantly for a girl, my dad told me I could be anything in the world except a daddy. Because of that confidence, it just didn't dawn on me that I couldn't do something."

Can you appreciate the difference in their outlook and expectations? It's not necessarily a poverty versus privilege dichotomy. If you look around at who is successful in leading the life they want and who is not, it becomes quickly apparent that the financial stability of your upbringing is no guarantee of your outcome. What – or whom, rather – does seem to play a significant role, however, is a great mentor.

I wonder how that young boy on the tricycle would react if, at 16, he was told that he could have, do, or be anything he seriously desired. That ethically and legally, he could create a brilliant life for himself? Would he believe it? It might depend on who told him. Often it takes a strong role model to challenge the long-held beliefs we have about ourselves.

A great mentor is someone who sees more in you than you do. They're holding a vision of what's possible for you until you can catch up and see it for yourself. "I think role models are the most important things that kids can have in their lives right now," says Olmos in that same documentary. And he's right. They are vitally important – for everybody. The right mentor gives you the ability to see what's available to you beyond what you've known in the past.

CHOOSING YOUR PATH: TUGI'S MISSION

Tugi Ryan Togiaheulu grew up in the lower class of Auckland, New Zealand, around gang culture. "I was a little rebel growing up," he says. "I could have easily gone down that path." Instead, Tugi chose to stay in school and eventually attended university. It was there, at 22, that he was introduced to Pablo Sinclair, who, like Tugi, had a real interest in supporting healthy community growth and connections. Each of the men, on their own, had launched what they considered to be *positive gangs* – safe, supportive groups interested in positive community development. The two – Tugi's Feel Good Buzz and Pablo's Happy Days – soon after joined forces to become #FGHD (Feel Good Happy Days).

Collectively, the members of this gang have made it their mission to improve the lives of people in their communities. There is no formal structure, forms to fill out, or membership fees to pay. Tugi and Pablo simply offer an open invitation for people to catch the spirit of positivity that they and their gang are promoting. Their first joint venture was an 8.4 km run, known as Round the Bays, touted as New Zealand's largest mass participation sporting event. Though it's a great opportunity for anyone to get some exercise and fresh air (and have a lot of fun doing it), the entry fees are cost-prohibitive for many in the community. So through corporate sponsorships, #FGHD raised the funds they needed to cover those fees for anyone who wanted to participate. "We had to hustle, but we've known how to hustle since we were little," grins Tugi. In the end, they drummed up enough support to pay for their team of 80 runners to participate and provide them with team shirts to boot.

Round the Bays has since become an annual event for #FGHD – their birthday celebration. In between those runs, you'll find #FGHD members organizing free exercise clinics, feeding families in need, taking kids out for paintball, kayaking, swimming, or supporting any number of other positive, feel-good activities to raise the energy and vibration of their communities. The gang culture they promote continues to spread, with events popping up throughout New Zealand, Australia, all through the Pacific and China. With an active social media presence, they're easy to reach out to.

What sort of environment did you grow up in? Were you told frequently that you could do anything you wanted with your life? Or did you experience indifference? Worse yet, were you exposed to a lot of negativity? Good, bad, or indifferent, all those experiences are part of your paradigm, and it's your paradigm that is controlling the results you're getting today.

So maybe you could not control your environment when you were younger, but you sure can now. Remember I mentioned in the introduction that early on, I thought that we had to play the cards we were dealt? Even if we didn't particularly care for them? Well, one of the cards I found consistently in my hand as a young adult was the shy and introverted one, and it held me back from a lot of things. On a conscious level, I imagined how wonderful it would be if I could be just a little more outgoing; if I had a little more confidence. I often thought about the people I could meet and the experiences I could have if I could just stand up and speak out. But I stayed put. Why? Remember, it's not our conscious mind that controls our actions – it's the deeply rooted paradigms that live in our *sub*conscious.

I love my mom. She was sweet and kind and generous. I am blessed and thankful to have had her in my life. She stayed at home and raised us, and I spent a lot of time with her. I could always count on her to help me feel secure, comforted, and loved. Outside our home, though, she was extremely shy. Unless she was with my dad, my mom was uncomfortable with – and so generally avoided – any situation that involved socializing with strangers.

So imagine, now, that I, as a child, am holding my mom's hand as we walk into a room full of strangers. How would she be feeling? Anxious, nervous even. Certainly anything but confident. And my young subconscious, of course, would readily pick up on that. Over time, that fear would become part of my paradigm. I began to associate groups of people I didn't know with feeling uncomfortable.

Let me clarify something important, though. This is *in no way* a blame game. A person simply cannot give you something they don't have. My mom could not share with me confidence and ease around groups of people if she did not possess those feelings herself. It didn't help her case that for much of her life, my mom lacked people in her close circle who could nurture in her a sense of confidence and capacity. But for me, thinking back on my childhood experiences gave me a window into where and how some aspects of my hand – the cards I was dealt – originated. Having recognized the contribution of these experiences to my paradigm, it was up to me to change those beliefs if I chose to do so.

When I began to travel around the country and then to other countries, presenting seminars and offering trainings, my mom would often remark that she could never do what I did. On many occasions, I tried to convince her that her statement was false. The truth was that she could – she just wasn't motivated to shift that part of her personality, her paradigm. To change something so deeply rooted, you've got to really want to. Boy did I want to!

Who we are is a blend of genetics (the traits and characteristics we inherited from our parents and ancestors) and our environmental conditioning. So while I may have an inherent introverted tendency, I wasn't prepared to let that define what I could or couldn't do. There are things that come more easily to you than other people, but the other side of the coin, of course, is that some things might present more of a challenge for you. This will sound crazy to some people, but I actually enjoy working with numbers, calculations, and financial statements. It comes easily to me. When it comes to learning languages? Not so much. But I have found that when a person wants to achieve something with their whole heart, they will find a way – regardless of their fears or perceived limitations.

How? Consider this: if you can see yourself already in possession of your goal, then you CAN achieve it. The reality is that if you can create the image on the screen of your mind and *really feel* that you have already attained the goal, *that's proof enough that you can do it*... even though you may not know how. Yet! You wouldn't be able to see the picture if you couldn't do it.

PUTTING AN END TO MENTAL MALPRACTICE

Let's look at how you can make a clear path to the achievement of your dream(s). Think about the top goals that you identified while reading the first section. It's time to weed out any negative beliefs you have about yourself that could be preventing you from making the choices you need to make and taking the actions you need to take to reach your goals.

The best way to begin is by simply listening to your self talk. When you close your eyes and get quiet, what do you hear? Do you talk to yourself throughout the day? Likely more than you realize. Some of us do it out loud (like my mom often did), but for the most part I mean the sort of talk that plays on repeat minute after minute, hour after hour, unconsciously. In his book *Beyond Hypnosis*, clinical psychologist Dr. Lee Pulos, Ph.D., points out that we self-talk at a rate of up to 1500 words per minute! "Our self-talk," he writes, "is our endless news broadcast about ourselves."

Is your self-talk predominantly positive or negative? Shad Helmstetter in his book *What to Say When You Talk to Yourself* reports that, on average, 77% of what we're saying is negative, counter-productive, and works against us. More than three-quarters! Does this resonate with you? If yes, then you too need to take control of your self-talk so that it becomes predominantly positive, productive, and useful!

Once you're really listening – once you've tuned into the playback loop of words, phrases, and ideas that you repeat over and over and over without even realizing it – start to figure out what you're hearing. What *do* you say when you talk to yourself? Try to witness it without getting involved with or upset by it. Just notice.

Here are a few examples of things you might hear:
* *I can't make a decision.*
* *I'm always late. I can't seem to show up on time. I'm always in a rush.*
* *I'm uncomfortable meeting and greeting people for the first time.*
* *I look awful. My (fill in the blank) just aren't good/nice/fit enough.*
* *I don't know enough/have enough experience to do what I want to do.*

Having heard all these things, it's likely that you can now identify some of the negative beliefs that you have been carrying with you and that are holding you back. It's up to you, now, to make some decisions.

What is the most pressing or overwhelming negative belief you have about yourself that you would like to change? And are you willing to do the work? It takes effort and will to make the shift, but if you consider how this belief has held you back in the past, the commitment might be easier to make. In my case, my shyness (the belief I held that meeting new people was scary and uncomfortable) resulted in missed opportunities, fewer friends and relationships, and less adventures. Until I did the work to release this deeply rooted negative belief I held, I would avoid networking opportunities and introducing myself to others, so those were some of the results of my actions, or *inactions,* as the case would be.

Once you've identified the belief you're ready to discard, write down what you consider to be its opposite in the form of something I call a

freedom statement. A freedom statement is a declaration you make about yourself, to yourself, while holding the image in your mind that you are already in possession of this goal. Start off with: "I am so happy and grateful now that...." and fill in the blank.

For example:
* *I am decisive. I easily make wise decisions and in a timely manner.*
* *I arrive on time, relaxed, calm and in control.*
* *I am confident meeting anyone, anytime, anywhere.*
* *I feel comfortable in my own skin.*
* *I realize I am enough. I have everything I need to succeed.*

Notice that these statements are always positive. Do not use negatives. You'll see I used the words *on time* as opposed to *not late*. Your mind can't focus on the reverse of an idea. Just like the old trick of saying: "Don't think of a pink elephant!" What's the image that comes up for you? Similarly, if I remind someone of something, I always say, "Please remember..." and not "Don't forget to..." The word *forget* seems to stick in their mind!

Just like writing down your goals, creating a freedom statement is a conscious exercise and therefore by itself will have not have any effect in bringing you a new result. At least not yet. This stage is like holding a new seed in your hand. It's something you know you want, but the seed has not yet received the warmth and water it needs to actually germinate.

As you sit quietly, just as you did when imagining yourself in possession of your goal, imagine that you are being or behaving just as you wish to be... just like the person you described in your freedom statement. In this moment of relaxation and awareness, bring in all the senses. Who else is with you? Where are you? Notice the colours, the smells. What do you hear? Feel what it feels like to be already in possession of that way of being.

Put this freedom statement (or a representative image of it) up on your vision board. Then, when you are visualizing daily what's up on your board, you are including this new image of yourself. It would be nice if we could make these positive statements really strongly, just one time, and have them stick, but unfortunately that's not quite the reality. Think about how long you've been listening to the negative statements – the loop of self-talk that puts you down and reinforces these unhelpful beliefs. It's likely been many, many years, and to be honest, you'll have probably become quite good at it. So you need some repetition of the new image. We'll take a closer look into how this works when we explore the **creative process.**

When I first wrote out my freedom statement of: "I am so happy and grateful now that I am calm and comfortable meeting anyone, anytime, anywhere," my conscious mind was incredibly excited about how cool that would be. Imagine! But it didn't take long for my subconscious belief system to crash the party. "Yeah, right," my self-talk began. "You're terrified. You'll never get over that. You may as well accept it. It's who you are." Did I manage to turn down the volume on that hindering self-talk? I sure did. But not overnight.

Understand that it has taken years of conditioning for you to become who you are today – beliefs and all. And so it takes time – often a lot of it – to fully integrate a new belief. When I was introduced to present one of my first seminars, I was still quaking in my boots at the thought of speaking in front of the massive audience that was awaiting my appearance onstage. But somehow, I knew, I *had* to figure out a way to force myself out in front of them. After all, they were *all* expecting me – all 18 of them. Today, I'm comfortable speaking with audiences of any size, but it was not always that way, and it's certainly been a process. But what freedom it has provided me!

When I was working through the process of changing my belief about meeting new people, it would have been a real blessing to have spent time with Tim Harris from Tim's Place Restaurant. This young man is a shining example of being comfortable with anyone, anytime, anywhere.

His father, Keith, describes just what I was aspiring to: "I'm endlessly fascinated with my adult study of Tim. It's my lifelong research project now – trying to learn from my son. In great waves of awareness, I'm understanding the wisdom that resides inside of him. One of the components of him that I totally admire is that when he meets someone for the first time, in any situation, he instinctively trusts them fully, and loves them fully. That's his starting point. Not just with some people, but with everyone he meets.

"We had deep philosophical discussions when he was younger with one of his teachers. She said she wanted to work on teaching him to *trust less*. And that triggered some thoughts in me. We had this wonderful discussion...

"'Please tell me,' I asked her, 'why we should teach this beautiful child to trust less?'

"'Well, he's going to get hurt if he trusts too much,' she replied.

"'But, Mary, you seem to be an incredibly intelligent woman and you, like me, have probably learned the appropriate amount of trust. Are you suggesting that you've never been hurt or burned?"

"'Well, of course not,' she admitted. 'I've been hurt many times in many amazing ways.'

"And this became the launching pad for our bigger discussion. What have you missed by holding yourself back? What's that loss? What does that add up to? You're going to get burned, but what magic happens if you accept people as they are and start from that place?"

As a result of Tim's ability to just *be* with people, he has encountered some really wonderful opportunities.

WELCOME TO THE PANIC ZONE!

An added benefit of you accomplishing something that exists well beyond your comfort zone – something like discarding or re-grooving some deeply rooted beliefs about yourself – is that you can begin to consider what other things you might like to do… things that you've previously talked yourself out of because of that, or another, limiting belief. I know that playing beyond your comfort zone can be super scary. But that's where life really starts – on that edge!

Imagine a person who is moving through life without any clear goals. They wake up each day and wonder what's going to happen. They perform their daily routine and they may experience some successes, but by their own admission, their life might be a four or five on a scale from one to 10. Then something causes them to take a real good look at what they're doing with their life, and they begin to imagine *what if? What if* they really could have, do, or be anything they want? *What if* they realize that they possess the capacity to make these changes all on their own? So they create a set of goals that would reflect their new life. Let's call it their Level 10 life.

A common mistake at this point is thinking (or hoping) that you can just keep doing what you've been doing in the past, aside from dreaming about this Level 10 life, and somehow expect these Level 5 actions to get you where you want to go. Can you achieve your Level 10 life doing what you've always done? Of course not. If that was the case, Level 10 would have shown up by now.

When we're operating somewhere in the Level 1 to Level 5 area of that scale, we're in our comfort zone. We may not be getting the results we want, but it's comfortable. There's little risk. But do you know what we achieve in our comfort zone? Not much. At least, not much more than we've done in the past. At best, you might see incremental improvements. At worst, things stay exactly the same or even decline.

This space is called our *comfort zone* because it describes a condition where our thoughts, feelings, and actions are all in sync. We are thinking thoughts, on a conscious level, that are in harmony with our subconscious conditioning, and we feel some degree of confidence and capability doing the actions we're doing to get the results we've more or less been accustomed to achieving. We can even begin to think thoughts on a conscious level about what our life would look like at a Level 10, but as long as we don't decide to make it happen and take action, we're still in that comfort zone. If we begin to take these Level 10 thoughts seriously, though, our discomfort starts to grow as we become frustrated about the gap between where we are and where we want to be.

So where do we have to play to achieve our Level 10? As scary as it sounds, this game takes place in what I call the *panic zone*; it's a space that feels *very* uncomfortable. Why? Because in order to act on a new idea (like speaking in front of an audience), you are trying to impress the new idea of who you are up against the old paradigm. You can expect some friction to occur.

When you are stepping out to act on a new idea that involves something you find scary, you begin to experience worry and doubt. This worry and doubt morph into an emotional state we know as fear, which soon enough manifests itself as anxiety in your body. This entire process can happen in milliseconds, and if you are unaware or lack the understanding of what's really happening in a situation like this, the most natural thing to do is retreat back to the home of those Level 5 ideas… where you're very comfortable. And once you're there, it's easy enough to come up with all sorts of justifications – excuses – for not pursuing the idea. It's so very tempting to run back to our comfort zone; it's so cozy and… unrewarding.

I'VE GOT $100 IN MY POCKET

During my first seminar series with Bob Proctor, Bob suggested that anyone who felt less than confident when meeting and greeting someone for the first time (I swear he was talking right to me) should carry a $100 bill in their pocket… always. That way, when you were in a situation that might bring up some anxiety – say a job interview or a sales call – you could reach into your pocket, find that bill, and know that you likely had more money in your pocket than they did in theirs.

It sounded good to me, and I was willing to try any trick or tool that would help me along. When I got home, I shared this idea with Karl, and the very next day he gifted me a brand new $100 bill. I put it in my pocket and carried it with me… for seven years. Yes, seven years! It was fun, it worked, and it felt good to know that I always had cash on hand

---

If you are willing to do only what's easy, life will be hard.
But if you are willing to do what's hard, life will be easy.
T. Harv Eker

A long-time friend of mine very successfully runs a construction company, so he also understands the value of having a stash of cash in your pocket. Over the years, I've gained some very valuable insights – on both a business level and a personal development level – from Ryan. He points out that while a business must be profitable, of course, to survive and prosper, the real purpose of any business is to help people grow. I like that perspective. And regardless of an employee's position in his company, Ryan always has an eye out for opportunities to help them have, do, and be more than they think they can. A great manager, friend, mentor or leader, remember, is someone who sees more in you than you see in yourself.

Ryan once gave Nancy, one of his employees, a $100 bill for the very reasons I just described. She was excited about this but a bit nervous, as it was out of her comfort zone to carry that much spare cash around. But after a few months, once Nancy became comfortable with the idea, Ryan turned up the heat. He handed her a $1,000 bill for her pocket. Or at least he tried to. She simply couldn't do it yet. $100 was a bit of stretch into her panic zone but $1,000? Nope. Not going to happen. Her paradigm did not allow for that level of prosperity, which was what Ryan was trying to help her develop. That experience had the opportunity to be a major ah-ha moment for Nancy.

EXPANDING YOUR COMFORT ZONE

Just like this employee refusing the $1000 bill, it would have been so much easier for me *not* to step out in front of that audience of 18 people. But I really, really, really wanted the goal of being able to do so with ease, so that pushed me through those uncomfortable feelings. Goals that we have fallen in love with do that for us. We learn to put up with the discomfort for the greater good.

The more we do this in different areas of our lives and in pursuit of various goals, we start to find that the panic zone doesn't have to be quite so *panicky* after all. It can become fun and exciting once we've gained the awareness (or understanding) that the massively uncomfortable feeling is *not* because of insufficient ability on our part. It can reflect a lack of experience but *not* lack of potential. It's essentially the result of you impressing your new image onto your old paradigm, and what you're feeling is the change that's taking place in your mind.

You've moved from your thoughts, feelings, and actions being in harmony (that was our definition of the comfort zone), to experiencing new ways of being that are – right now – foreign to you. When you feel you're in the panic zone, it's a great sign. "That's good," you can learn to tell yourself. "It means I'm on track." Stay the course and you will absolutely experience rewards that others sit comfortably and wish for.

Here's the best part: as you expand past the outer reaches of your comfort zone, over and over again, the edges – slowly but surely – begin to blur. What was once your panic zone becomes part of your new, expanded comfort zone. **That's called personal growth!** So the next time you step out to act on a new idea and you feel that doubt, fear, and anxiety bubble up, don't stop! Now you know to recognize the feeling of your old paradigm intersecting with new ideas and experiences, and instead of running from it, sit with it. Stay. Acknowledge the yappy puppy, gently remind it to quiet down, and continue on… wobbly knees and all.

There's no doubt that it's hard to move beyond your comfort zone. But the benefits far, far outweigh the temporary discomfort if you stay the course. Imagine what your life will be like! It takes courage. It takes guts. It takes goals. It's scary, but it's beautiful. It's like climbing a mountain. As you journey upwards, your view continues to expand outward. You can see farther with each step, and the scenery just keeps getting better and better. And then you get to see what's next.

CHAPTER FIVE

NEW HABITS. NEW YOU. NEW RESULTS.

The next step is to begin forming the good habits you need to achieve your goals, since the results you have in your life right now are largely due to your habitual way of being. You likely already know some of the things you'd like to change. We've talked about goals and beliefs about yourself and your world. So put it all on the table now. Don't hold back. Don't limit yourself. My hope is that you will discover a goal big, bold, and beautiful enough – a goal you truly desire with your whole head and heart – that it will make you want to take these big steps out of your comfort zone and toward your Level 10 life. And trust me... once you find something that you want badly enough, you'll make it happen. What is that for you?

"There is a vitality, a life force, an energy, a quickening that is translated through you into action, and because there is only one of you in all of time, this expression is unique," said modern dance pioneer Martha Graham. "And if you block it, it will never exist through any other medium and it will be lost. The world will not have it."

No one has your unique set of talents and abilities that will allow you to live your own individual purpose. No one can make the contribution you can, in the way that you are able. You are so very unique. So let's begin to set aside the self-limiting beliefs, the negative self-talk, and all thoughts of doubt and worry, and let your inner Golden Buddha shine!

Focus on developing the beneficial habits you want and less on the habits you need to let go of. For example, for all of us, our days are pretty full – we are creatures of habit. But that doesn't *necessarily* mean productive... just habitual. If you've made the decision to pursue a new goal, then you'll need to find the time to work on it. You'll need to let go of something you're doing now to create space for the new. That might mean cutting back on the time you spend gaming, or sleeping, or scrolling through social media. But don't look at it as giving something up. In truth, you are trading something of less value for something with more value.

Successful people have successful habits. Intuitively, you already know what changes you need to make to encourage the start or growth of those successful habits. And fortunately, the variety of resources many of us have access to is immense – the world wide web, local libraries, teachers, mentors. For nearly anything you need to improve on, there are tools out there to help you too; think time management, stress management, dealing with difficult people or assertive communication skills. And, in lots of cases, chances are... there's an app for that!

The biggest hurdle is building the will to do it – whatever *it* is. As a reminder of this, one of the notes taped to the edge of my computer screen reads: "If it is to be, it's up to me." There are many facets of your life that you can delegate, but when it comes to your personal development, health, and well-being, it's up to you. Unfortunately, you can't hire someone to do your workout or cultivate your more enriching habits.

If there are a few habits you have in mind you'd like to change, focusing on one at a time is a good idea. It would be great to integrate them all tomorrow, but that often leads to overload, frustration, and giving up. Instead, choose the one that you consider to be the most pressing and work on it. Create a freedom statement to support that new behaviour and actively make it part of your daily life.

THE COMPANY YOU KEEP

Make your transformation and your new reality easier to manifest by surrounding yourself with positive influences. Consider the five people you interact with the most. Are they positive, happy, and productive? Do they often talk about how things can be done and what's working? Or are they whiners, complainers, and generally negative individuals who are quick to point out what's not working and who's to blame? The people in the latter group are not necessarily bad people, but they're operating from a certain paradigm. And it's more than likely that they aren't fully aware of the detrimental impact they are having on themselves and those around them.

You'll discover that as you integrate more of these ideas into your life, you will spend less and less time with people like that. It happens quite organically. As you become more aware and respectful of your inner essence (your higher self) and begin to cultivate a deeper understanding of what you are really capable of, you won't want to spend any time around negative people. It will feel a bit like trying to blend oil and water. As you're thinking about your goals and visualizing yourself already in possession of your future self, you will start to become emotionally invested in these ideas. That, in turn, changes your vibratory rate. So what you begin to attract to yourself (including people) will be quite different. I guarantee you, the rich and successful people I know do not spend their days talking about why things can't be done!

> The people around you have an amazing impact on your view of life. When you surround yourself with positive, self-confident people, you become positive and self-confident.
> **Bud Bilanich, E.D., The Common Sense Guy**

You may find that you increasingly have less in common with some of the people you used to spend time with, and a few of them might not like who you are becoming. And that's okay, because you'll also find that you begin to attract new friends and acquaintances who are more in harmony with where you are going in your life. As for toxic relatives? Don't visit as often, and don't stay as long.

PERSISTENCE PAYS: ZACHARY'S TALE

For a variety of reasons, high school was not an easy time for Australian Zachary Rook. He dreamed of financial prosperity, in part so he could purchase his dream car – a Maserati or Lamborghini – but seemed to keep getting into the wrong sort of activities. He was headed down the wrong path, and he knew it. To keep himself out of trouble, Zachary dived into the local break-dancing scene, and eventually began organizing and running dance events after school. There was something in the music, something about the kind of rising-up-from-the-gutters hip-hop story-telling that resonated with him. The music spoke and Zachary listened.

"They were rapping about how you can do it… how you can go and make money, do what you want to do," he says. "The music reminds you to dream about the things you want to do."

He admits that these positive messages were probably his first experience with self-improvement and encouraged him to pursue his goals at a time when he was struggling to stay on his path to success. "One of my big reasons for really wanting to push dancing," he admits, "was that I saw the impact it had on me when I was in a potentially make or break situation: getting suspended, getting arrested, all that. It wasn't that I was a particularly bad kid. I knew I was doing the wrong stuff, but I was just bored and had no outlet and neither conventional schooling nor the school environment was at all helpful."

It was during one of these dance events that he happened to strike up a conversation with a dance teacher from New Zealand. "I'd met the guy once for a couple of hours and knew immediately that was what I wanted to do. If I am really serious, I remember thinking, that's where I need to go." So at 19, Zachary packed his bags and hopped on a plane to New Zealand to study with this teacher.

It was there that the young dancer found himself a few months later, cash-strapped and in search of a job – any job at all – that would financially enable him to continue with his training. He signed on with a moving company and lasted all of four hours on the job before he recognized an opportunity to do something bigger and better. He borrowed $3,500 to buy a truck and was in business. Although he had originally planned on using his dance training to help other at-risk youth find better outlets for their energy, Zachary instead made a point of hiring these same youths for his new business. In doing so, he could help them raise their self-worth and attitude toward both themselves and the world around them.

After less than a year of building up the business to include five vehicles and all the required movers, Zachary and his business partner decided it was time to make the move back to Brisbane. Zachary stayed and dismantled his company, sold off all the assets, and sent the money to his business partner, who had gone on ahead to re-establish the business in its new location; ideally it would be up and running when Zachary arrived. What he found when he returned, though, was not a functioning business but an empty bank account. His partner had done nothing but squander every bit of the funds they had spent the last year accumulating.

No success story is without obstacles, and many an entrepreneur has lost it all at some point only to build it all back up, bigger and better than before. Once Zachary had managed to re-establish himself, the business again took off. *Your Local Movers* grew, on average, 120% annually for the next three years. By 2010, Zachary's boyhood dreams of success seemed well on their way to actualizing: he had just signed a lease on a new 2,500 square metre premises, and there was a defence contract in the works that was going to be a cornerstone of their growth strategy. They moved into their new space in December of 2011. Less than a month later, thanks to record-breaking Brisbane floods, the entire place was 15 feet (4.46 metres) under water.

Zachary and his team managed to save all the clients' stored possessions by moving them into company vehicles and parking those on hills in the surrounding area. They did this despite Your Local Movers *not* being legally liable for their clients' possessions. "It was just the right thing to do," explained Zachary. Unfortunately, their own supplies and equipment had only been moved up to the mezzanine level, a mere 10 feet above ground.

It was a tremendous amount of work, but the team got the mess cleaned up and moved back into the facility in March. That was already a lot for anyone to deal with, let alone a 22-year-old entrepreneur. But there was still more to come. Over the next few months, power on the street turned on and off intermittently due to damage to the city's infrastructure caused by the flooding. One Saturday in August, the power once again went out about an hour before closing, so Zachary decided to call it a day. He made a reservation at a local restaurant for himself and some friends and went home to change before heading out to dinner.

"The restaurant was about 10 minutes away from the office and storage depot," he explains. "I got to the front door and was dropping someone off before I parked. Our security company called me then, and I kind of got a funny feeling. Occasionally, the alarm goes off for no reason – a bird flies into a window or whatever – but I listened to that funny feeling. I left the restaurant and drove straight to the depot. By the time I got there, it was gone. Ten minutes after the alarm had gone off, there were flames five feet above the roof."

It was an electrical fault. The electrician had failed to rewire one crucial wall that was roughly a metre and a half long. It was the *only* wall not completely redone after the flood. The storage depot, thanks to Zachary's ability to re-build their business, was completely full of client goods. "The fire totally destroyed everything," he admits, "including me."

A few days later – what Zachary describes as one of the worst days of his life – they sat down and called every last customer to tell them that all of their stored possessions had been destroyed. The company lost just under a million dollars that year, and they were completely out of cash. But Zachary still didn't give up. It's been a long haul to get back on their feet, but *Your Local Movers* have indeed returned to the road, and the business is, yet again, growing.

In 2011, Zachary joined the local chapter of the Entrepreneurs

Organization looking for support and guidance after experiencing so many setbacks. The EO is open to entrepreneurs and founders of businesses making more than US$1 million in annual revenue and who meet the values of the organization. "It was probably the thing that kept me going through the next three years," he says. "The disasters were tough, but with the help of my mentors I was able to remodel the business, expand locations, and improve technology processes, so it's onwards and upwards from here!"

Sometimes the path to your goals is rocky, bumpy, and unclear. But keeping the larger goal in mind, accepting positive support from mentors, and staying focused will allow you to continue the journey. As in Zachary's case, events don't always play out as we expect, but the universe often surprises us with bigger and better results than we could have imagined. So how do you stand strong amid the unfolding of chaos? You need a plan, a roadmap. To get from start to finish, and successfully navigate any unexpected obstacles in between, you need to follow the **creative process**.

CHAPTER SIX

IF YOU CAN HOLD IT IN YOUR HEAD, YOU CAN HOLD IT IN YOUR HAND!

THE CREATIVE PROCESS

Years ago I had the opportunity to purchase a delicatessen in the small mountain city to which I had recently re-located. My partner and I purchased it for basically the cost of the existing equipment. Aside from that, there was no real value as it was an operation that was quickly going out of business. Needless to say, a number of people thought it was a crazy idea, especially when neither of us had any culinary or food service experience. But I like to eat. I figured that was a good enough reason to proceed. That, and it felt like a great opportunity. I viewed it as a turnaround project. And believe me, it needed a lot of turning around… about 180 degrees worth. I'll use the example of rebuilding the deli to help describe **the creative process**. This 7-step process, described below, was used to obtain financing and complete the deal. Then it was time to apply the same methodology again to create prosperity within the business.

FROM DREAMING TO MANIFESTING: THE 7 CRITICAL STEPS

Step 1: Imagine.

As you know well by this point, everything starts with an idea. Look around and remember that everything you see began, at some point, as a single thought in someone's mind. Using one of our six intellectual factors, the imagination, we begin to dream of what we would like to have, do, or be. In the case of the deli, it was vital that we build an image on the screen of our mind of what we wanted it to be in the future, and discard the image of what it actually was – a business in desperate need of fixing.

Step 2: Do your homework.

We've talked about how people often make the mistake of believing some version of the story: "I'd like to do that, but I can't because I don't have the money." A lesson instilled in me long ago by Bob Proctor is that you don't need the money until you make the decision to go ahead with whatever you need the money for. And it's not just a saying. That order is critical.

Always, always, always take a look at the deal first. Does it make sense to you? Is it a good investment? Do your due diligence FIRST, and if you give it a green light, *that's* when you start the process of attracting the money you'll need. One day I was in the Chamber of Commerce office with an acquaintance, discussing various businesses and buildings that were for sale. I noticed a bed & breakfast that was listed for $800,000 and pointed it out. "Wow, that's too expensive," she said immediately. I thought that was an interesting belief, as it had just come on the market, and I knew she wasn't familiar with the property. How could she know it was too expensive? Maybe it was, or maybe it was the deal of the decade! Her paradigm caused her to reject the opportunity simply because of the price, without knowing more about the property or the revenue it had been generating.

When the founder of Transcendental Meditation, Maharishi Mahesh Yogi, was asked where the money would come from for a massive event he was planning – one that would attract hundreds of thousands of people and share TM with the world – his answer was brilliant. "From wherever it is now," he said. There are trillions and trillions of dollars in circulation today; as long as you're providing a service, why shouldn't some of that be utilized by you?

Our first decision was to purchase the deli. During that process, we worked at gaining clarity as to what success at this new business would mean. What would it look like? What images did we need to hold?

Step 3: See it. Feel it.

In that relaxed state you're becoming accustomed to adopting, see yourself in your mind's eye already in possession of the good you desire. Really feel it as though it's happening right now. Feel the gratitude you have for living your dream. As you do, you are turning it over to the treasury of your subconscious mind.

I had to train myself so that when I thought of the deli, the new image of an establishment full of happy customers and the sweet sound of the cash register came to mind, rather than the one that my senses were showing me at the time. Most of us are gifted with five sensory factors – we can hear, see, smell, taste and touch. These allow us to connect with our physical world as it is, in any given moment. Using these sensory factors alone, I saw the state of the business – a quiet, unprofitable shop with few customers. Without a new image, I would have continued to see and feel this, and thus would have continued creating more of the same.

You must develop your *will*, which you recall is one of your six intellectual factors. It gives you the ability to hold the image in your mind and stay focused on that picture, rather than allowing yourself to be knocked off course by external circumstances.

Step 4. Stay in tune with your goals.

By visualizing what you want, you become in tune with the good you desire, and by doing so, you are tapping into an infinite source of supply. But what is this source? It's known by many names, and you might have a preference for a particular term. If we turn to science, we are told that there is a power that permeates and penetrates the entire cosmos. It's equally present in all places at all times. It has no beginning and no end. It flows through everyone and everything. It's called energy. If we turn to theology, we are told that there is a power that permeates and penetrates the entire cosmos. It's equally present in all places at all times. It has no beginning and no end. It flows through everyone and everything. It's called God or a whole host of other names. You can see that the name you give it is less important than your conscious awareness of your connection with all that is. What does this mean for your goals and the achievement of them? Let's take a closer look at this quote from *Your Invisible Power* that I shared with you in Act 1:

*"When your understanding grasps the power to visualize your heart's desire and hold it with your will, it attracts to you all things requisite to the fulfillment of that picture by the harmonious vibrations of the law of attraction... **Everyone visualizes, whether they know it or not. Visualizing is the great secret of success.** The conscious use of this great power attracts to you multiplied resources, intensifies your wisdom, and enables you to make use of advantages which you formerly failed to recognize."*

VISUALIZATION & ATTRACTION

Recognize that everything is energy. As such, everything moves, or you could say, vibrates. From our mental thoughts to the most solid form of matter, everything is in a state of vibration.

Your hand, for example, appears quite solid. But it is, in fact, a mass of molecules at a high speed of vibration; with the right equipment, you could actually see the particles of energy moving.

When you hold the image of the good that you desire on the screen of your mind, in a relaxed (or even meditative) state, you are moving into a vibratory rate that is in harmony with everything that is necessary for the manifestation of your image on the physical plane. You become in tune with the good you desire. Your job is to stay at that level of vibration as much as possible. How? By falling in love with your image *so much* that it becomes a part of you. You act like the person already in possession of your goal, and it becomes your new habitual way of thinking. This is where the vision board becomes such a powerful tool because you are dedicating time each day to move into that vibration and, to the best of your ability, stay there. It means being, thinking, feeling, and acting like the person you want to be. In other words, *fake it 'til you make it*. (But, by doing this, on many levels you *have* made it).

Another powerful tool that I use often is an audio recording, in my own voice, of the freedom statements and goals on my vision board. It's so easy today to record and add background music. When I first started doing this, I was using a plastic cassette tape! Today, I have these recordings on my smartphone that I listen to every morning when I first wake up. Try this! It's a simple but effective way to put yourself into a wonderful vibration, from which you can launch into the rest of your day.

If and when you get knocked off course during the day, at the very least you have this time each morning to get centred and bring yourself back on course. Even though our deli had few customers at the time, I built a beautiful image on the screen of my mind, which included seeing the space filled with happy customers, feeling the high energy level in the shop, and being so very grateful it was *the* happening place in town to come for lunch!

KEEP GROWING YOUR VISION

At the time that we bought the deli, there certainly were a few business owners in my community whose conversations seemed to centre around how awful the economy was and how difficult it was to run a profitable business at that time. It felt like they had a disease I didn't want to catch… so I stayed away as much as possible. They were very justified in their views; they could cite statistics and news coverage that proved their point – things were bad! But that line of thinking simply wasn't helpful for me. It was, in fact, the polar opposite of the image I had for our business. If you know people like this, RUN as fast as you can in the opposite direction. They would love to have you join their pity party.

Know that for any goal you set, there can be lots of reasons why it won't work… but know too that there are also always reasons why it can. Once you commit to the decision that this is something you want to go for, don't spend *any* mental energy focusing on why it won't work. Instead, talk about how it CAN be done. By holding tight to the image of the positive outcome we wanted, my partner and I began to see ways to make that happen. And so instead of staying in town worrying about the state of things, we went to trade shows in major cities to find out what was hot and happening in the food world. I've been involved in a few different industries, and I must say that the food shows were by far my favourite. A day of work there involves visiting all the booths and taste-testing all day. Tough job! As a result, we were the first deli in our town to offer things like frozen yogurt, pizza by the slice, and we-make-you-bake pizzas. These may seem far from earth-shattering ideas, but things like this continually brought more and more people to our place, and it was heaps of fun to build the business.

Step 5: Listen to your intuition.

Being connected with the good that you desire on a deeper level will not deliver this image to your doorstep. But what that connection *does* do is begin to reveal insights and ideas for us to notice and pursue. There are two times in the day that I seem to receive the most pure inspirations and ideas. The first is at the start of my day as I begin to stir from sleep, when I'm still quiet, relaxed, and in a deep meditative state. As I move out of this and become more fully awake, the paper and pen next to the bed is very handy to capture whatever ideas appear. Sometimes I even use the dictation app on my phone! The second is during my morning walk. For me, being active outdoors first thing in the morning seems to be highly conducive to receiving inspirations.

Hunches or intuitive hits will also come to you as a result of the help from your reticular activating system (RAS), which heightens your sensitivity to important information. This network of nerve fibres, found at the base of your brain, is located deep within the brain stem and helps regulate the brain's level of awareness. Sensory messages that pass through the brainstem stimulate the RAS, which in turn stimulates activity and alertness throughout the cerebral cortex. The RAS acts as a filter. At any given moment, you are surrounded by thousands of stimuli: sights, sounds, scents, and images that you couldn't possibly absorb all on a conscious level. This filtering system brings to your attention those stimuli *that are important to you at any given time.*

Even a very simple room in your house, for example, is filled with stimuli – what's on the floors, anything hanging on the walls, the colours in the room, even the lighting. When I walk into a room, I'm quick to spot any fresh flowers that might be around. In the past, I owned a flower shop (where we sold upwards of 11,000 carnations every week!), and I love them – so I tend to notice flowers. But for my friend Joel – 18 years a professional visual artist – his gaze would slide right over the flowers and instead be focused on any and all paintings. He notices art! Remember, your RAS filters stimuli based on what's important to *you*... not anyone else.

Maybe in the past, you've bought a vehicle. You drive it off the lot or away from its previous owner, and as you're making your way down the street, you begin to notice how many other people are driving the same type of vehicle as you! They were there before, but that make, model, and colour of vehicle likely wasn't important to you – until you owned one. It just wasn't on your radar. And this applies across the board. What things are you noticing today?

By going through your mindful morning routine, you are quite literally sending messages to your brain and the rest of your body about what is important to you right now. As your RAS accommodates that information and begins to draw your attention to relevant people, things, and ideas in the world around you, your job is to figure out how you can follow the insights that appear. You'll see an ad for a trade show you need to be at or overhear a conversation that triggers a solution to a problem you're having. Even though there's been incredible advances in science and technology over the past century, we are still just scratching the surface of discovering and tapping into our innate capabilities for producing real shifts in the world we inhabit. Start to build your awareness of what the universe offers you when you really, truly ask. You'll be amazed.

Step 6: Act.

It's a real gift to receive these ideas and insights, but more is required than simply acknowledging them and giving thanks. You *must* act on them. After you've built the image of what you'd like to have, do, or be, and you've really put it out there to the universe, you'll begin to receive insights that point you to the next step. That's when you act. It's as if you have an agreement with the universe, and it's your duty to keep up your end of the bargain… the action end. The action is how you say: "Thanks, I hear you. I'm on it."

Blaming a poor economy, deli after deli around us closed their doors. With the exception of just one other, we were the only remaining business of that type in town after only a few years. Our economy, it seemed, was just fine! Even during times of potent economic devastation – the Great Depression, for example – there were people who continued to bring in millions of dollars. Just because your town, city, province, state or country is encountering financial difficulty, *you do not have to buy into that story* unless you choose to, unconsciously or otherwise. You can *always* choose prosperity if you're willing to do the work that allows that to be possible.

Step 7: Repeat.

Once your vision has become your reality, go back to step one and repeat the process. What's another idea you'd like to pursue? What is it you would like to create in your world?

THE POWER OF A SINGLE THOUGHT

"I'd like you to remember one thing," said Greek-American musician Yanni, live on stage at the Acropolis. "Everything great that has ever happened to humanity since the beginning began as a single thought in someone's mind. And if any one of us is capable of such a great thought, then all of us have the same capacity and capability because we are all the same."

In addition to the live audience who witnessed his performance that day, more than a billion people have since seen this recorded concert. And it was the manifestation of a fierce dream for Yanni (born Yiannis Chryssomallis), who, since his childhood, had dreamt of returning to his homeland to play music for his people.

The pianist – who had never learned to read or write music in the traditional sense but instead created his own shorthand version – left Greece at 18 to attend university in the United States. After earning a BA in psychology, Yanni still yearned for a musical career. But getting exposure was difficult; his music was instrumental, he toured with a large, expensive orchestra, and he didn't sing. The biggest problem, he knew, was that mainstream avenues like music television and radio were essentially closed to him. So Yanni gave himself a period of time to solve the problem.

Anytime you embark on something new, barriers will appear. You'll think of many reasons – or your friends, family, and even strangers will – as to why it just won't work. Coming up with a list of those is pretty easy. But remember, once you decide to do something – anything – there's no value in expending any mental effort talking about why it won't work. That's because if you're really good, which many of us are, you may even talk yourself out of pursuing your dream!

Drop all that. If you've decided to forge ahead, focus all your attention on how you CAN. Not why you can't. Yanni did just that.

For the entirety of one year, he decided, he would commit 100% of his time, energy, and capacity to musical success. First on the agenda was figuring out how to get his music heard.

His breakthrough came when he managed to snag a spot on *The Oprah Show*, an appearance which gave him just what he needed – great exposure. Thousands and thousands of viewers who saw that segment flocked to music shops to find copies of his work for their own collections. His musical career, in its full glory, was born.

This same power of focus and determination worked for Yanni again when he committed to making his return to Greece a reality. More than two decades after his exodus, the musician set out to organize a live performance at the 2000-year-old Herodes Atticus Theater at the Acropolis of Athens. With no network yet committed to air the footage, Yanni poured absolutely everything he had – nearly $2 million – into arranging and recording the event. Thankfully, PBS got on board; the network eventually aired it multiple times as part of its fundraising program. The rest, as they say, is history.

Yanni, Live at the Acropolis became the second best-selling music video of all time after Michael Jackson's *Thriller*. And he and his accomplishments are as unique as his music. In 1997, Yanni became one of the few Western artists permitted to perform and record at the Taj Mahal in India, as well as the first Western artist to perform at the Forbidden City in Beijing, China. During a Chinese TV appearance, he joked that if *Live at the Acropolis* had not been financially successful, it would have been one of the most expensive home videos ever made. And as the musician said in a recent interview: "It all started as a single thought."

CHAPTER SEVEN

TAKE CONTROL

OF YOUR THINKING (AND YOUR LIFE!)

To develop a strong belief in yourself, you <u>must</u> take control of your thinking. It's not an option. Otherwise, you'll be at the mercy of whatever is happening around you. "He upset me," you may have heard yourself say. "She made me angry."
Are those true statements?

They are easy excuses for our own behaviours, but they're also completely unproductive, inaccurate, and even harmful. The reality is that we take on what *he* or *she* says and internalize it. This produces our reaction. Anger. Disappointment. Fear. In this way, we pass the reins; we admit that this other person has full control over our state of mind and how we feel. We abandon responsibility for our well-being by giving it away.

Do you remember that a belief is our evaluation of something? And that we're free to re-evaluate our beliefs about just about anything? Let's do some re-evaluating with the intent of cleansing our thinking and allowing us a faster track to goal achievement.

SET LIMITS

If this is a person you feel you want or need to continue a relationship with, maybe a co-worker or family member, you'll want to set limits with them about what you will or will not tolerate. Whether we realize it or not, we *do* train people how to treat us through the way we react to them. If someone is in the habit of yelling at you, and in the past you've put up with it, you've been sending the message that they can continue that behaviour.

There's lots of good material out there on assertive communication skills and dealing with difficult people that you can turn to for the nuts and bolts of how to maintain your centre and deal with these people effectively. Having said that, as you continue to study *yourself* and challenge your belief systems and habits, you'll be amazed at how these sorts of people show up in your world less and less.

BE INTROSPECTIVE

What triggered you? Is the topic at hand a hot button one for you? Why? Whatever *they* did or said, was there something inside *you* that caused the negative reaction? Imagine you and I are out for dinner. "I think you're a lousy friend," I say. How will you respond? Your reaction will be based on how you perceive yourself. If you know deep down that you're actually an awesome friend, my comment would have no effect on you, aside from potentially shortening our dinner date. You might just look at *me* differently and assume that I have a perception problem. If you've been feeling guilty, though, about the lack of time you've been spending with friends of late, my comment might trigger that guilt, and you might feel terrible. If that's the case, then you need to adjust your calendar, your belief, or maybe a bit of both!

If your negative reaction is rooted in your own insecurity or doubt, consider viewing an encounter like that as an opportunity to create a freedom statement. Begin to rid yourself of that limiting belief, whatever it is. Otherwise, the issue will surely surface again.

Everything can be taken from a person except one thing – the last of all human freedoms – the ability to choose one's attitude in any given situation... to choose one's own way.
Viktor Frankl, *Man's Search for Meaning*

THE CONSEQUENCE OF BLAMING OTHERS

Remember that what you are attracting in your life is a result of your vibration. Moment by moment, day by day, you bring it in. The thoughts that dominate your psyche, driven by your subconscious conditioning, are what dictate your vibration. Are those thoughts positive or negative? Do they cheer you on or criticize you or the world around you? Once you really grasp how powerful your thoughts can be and the effect they have on your results, you will start paying very close attention to what's going on in there. You will cease badmouthing yourself and others because you will understand how much harm that does you.

The universe is quite unconcerned with your awareness of its rules. They're always at work. The law of gravity, for example, doesn't cease to operate if you don't understand how it works. The apple will still fall from the tree when it's ready, even if you happen to be standing below. Similarly, you may know someone in your life who is clearly their own worst enemy. They are unhappy with the world around them, and bad luck seems to keep showing up for them. Imagine their reaction if you suggested that maybe, just maybe, they had a significant role in attracting all that? It's far easier to blame others – external forces – than to take responsibility ourselves. But once we do... it works both ways. The sky's the limit.

During my *Winning the Money Game* seminar, I often share the story of a woman who once attended a class with me in Biloxi, Mississippi. I was in the midst of explaining how our financial situation is a direct result of the paradigm we craft, carry, and feed, and for any chance at long-term stable wealth, we *must* alter that paradigm to one that is in harmony with the abundance we seek.

When we start to talk about money, I always like to have my clients, participants, or students consider how their parents handled financial matters. Were they spenders or savers? Was money a positive or negative topic of conversation in the household when you were growing up?

"I grew up in a household where my dad made most of the financial decisions," this particular woman shared with the seminar group. "From a young age, I was working part-time, saved money, and by the time I left home at age 22, I had $10,000 in my bank account. Soon after, I met a man I thought was Mr. Right. When that relationship ended barely a year and a half later, that account was empty, and I was in debt for $7,000."

In that relationship, who do you think was looking after the finances? Mr. Wrong, of course. Why? Because that was the environment this woman was raised in, and she was all too willing to allow the man in the relationship to take on that role. Sadly, it took two more similar occurrences with two more men for her to realize that blaming them for her financial loss was not the solution.

She could certainly feel very justified in holding a bundle of resentment against all three men, but it would do nothing to prevent it from happening again. Once this woman came to the realization that she needed to step up and take responsibility for the money situation herself, she was well on her way to regaining her financial freedom. She re-evaluated her situation, and her belief about her situation changed.

LIGHTENING YOUR MENTAL LOAD

It's easy to say and harder to do, but the ability to *let go* is essential – of negative ideas, beliefs, interactions, experiences or patterns. If we can't release the mistakes we've made in the past – yesterday, last week, last month, years ago – we'll never move forward with the confidence and positivity that we deserve and require to be successful in creating the future we desire. If you can't let go of resentment, anger, and guilt, you'll never experience real peace of mind.

Professional athletes know about letting go. They have to practise it regularly. If you've ever watched any competitive performance, you've surely seen crashes, falls, failures, losses... So then what? Athletes have to get up, brush themselves off, and continue with the game/performance/race… whatever it is they're working at. Otherwise, what happens? You've probably seen it; they fall, crash, or fail again. You can generally tell when someone hasn't let go of their first mistake because it quite literally trips them up again.

Using our orange tree analogy, we can see that the seed, roots, trunk, branches, and fruit of a tree are all connected. In the same way, our mind, body, and results are connected – what we think, what we do, and what comes of it. Imagine an athlete trying to propel their body forward while they're mentally still back at the fall. It just doesn't work. So too for you and I off the sporting field. If we are trying to move forward in our lives but our mind is rooted back to our perceived injustices or mistakes of the past, we will certainly trip ourselves up. *Let the past be a guide, not a hitching post.* Learn from it and move on. Or, as my precocious niece (at the ripe age of six) told her frazzled mother when a quick stop at a traffic light caused the contents of a pizza box to pile up in a heap... "Put the cheese back on the pizza, and MOVE ON WITH YOUR LIFE!"

THE TWO MOST DESTRUCTIVE EMOTIONS

Resentment and guilt are two of the worst things to involve yourself in. Holding on to the idea of these past injustices is simply reinforcing their detrimental effects each time you relive them.

Guilt is about something you said or didn't say, something you did or didn't do... and every time you revisit the idea, you move into the negative vibration that it carries. Resentment is about something *someone else* said or didn't say, something they did or didn't do, and the same principle applies. Every time you relive this injustice, you take on that negative vibration again. Do you see the similarity here? Guilt is directed at you and resentment toward someone else. But regardless of the source, note that you are the one who experiences the dangerous effects of recounting it over and over!

A person who is truly aware of the power of their thoughts and these universal laws will not engage in these emotions long-term. Consider what you feel guilty about. Whatever it is, know that you did the best you could at the level of awareness you had available at the time. It's where you were in your evolution. And, since it happened in the past and you can't change it, you may as well accept it. Accept that the situation played out the way it did, and THAT'S OKAY. Since that time, you've grown, and now you would handle things differently. Internalize the lesson that you've gained from that experience, and release the guilt. Be grateful that you can view the situation from a different vantage point today.

Resentment, like guilt, is a negative idea you are holding on to about an event that happened in the past, but in this case that negativity is directed at someone else. But once again, you are the unwilling benefactor of the energy you're stuck in. Holding a resentment, I once heard from someone very clever, is like drinking poison, and expecting someone else to take ill.

Consider it this way: though both guilt and resentment are emotions tied to past events, we often continue to harbour them today – in the present – which is the only time we know FOR CERTAIN that we have available. Of course, I would like to believe that each and every one of us will live a very long and fulfilling life. But the reality is that none of us really knows how much time we actually have.

TIME IS A GIFT: BE HERE NOW

I was windsurfing once off a beach in the Cayman Islands. Toward the end of the week, the wind began to quiet down, so I switched to scuba diving while I waited for it to return. During my few days of diving, I befriended Phil, a man from Miami who was visiting the islands with his wife and two young kids. The youngest child, although eager, was too young to dive, and Phil's wife wasn't certified either, so the two of them would come for the boat ride and snorkel around the surface while the divers descended to explore the underwater world of the sea.

The group of us had a fantastic time together. Relaxing on the boat and heading back to shore at the end of day two, Phil commented that he would see me tomorrow. This surprised me, as he knew the wind was picking up, and I was planning on returning to my board. As it turns out, his family had talked him into trying windsurfing for the first time, so he had arranged to take a lesson the next morning. This was great news! It's an incredibly fun sport.

Later that evening, my partner and I drove into the nearby town, Georgetown, for dinner. We had a wonderful night but didn't stay out too late; we both wanted to hit the water, wind, and waves early the next morning. Georgetown is at one end of the island, and our hotel was at the other. Since the whole island is just over 20 miles across, the trip is really quite short... usually. There is a north route and south route, each with just one lane in each direction. We chose the south route to take us home, and part way there we came upon an accident. Officials at the scene told us it would be a while before the road was opened up again and suggested that we turn around and take the north route. So we did.

When I arrived the next day at the windsurfing hut, I looked around for Phil but didn't see him or his family around, which I thought was quite odd. They (and we) were all pretty stoked about watching Dad tackle the wind and waves for the first time. I started to ask around, and, to my immense sadness, I soon discovered that it was Phil and his family who were involved in that accident. On Grand Cayman, people drive on the left hand side of the road. In Miami, they drive on the right.

The body is an instrument of the mind. It acts and moves according to the thoughts we entertain. Do you remember when you learned how to drive? Every bit of conscious attention was required to drive the vehicle and keep it on the road. I have a vivid memory of learning to drive on a country road and reaching over on my right to change the radio station, and all of a sudden I felt the entire vehicle make its way far into the right shoulder. My 16-year-old body wasn't skilled enough yet to handle that simple additional task! At first, driving a vehicle requires your full attention. But then you repeat the task of driving over and over and over again. We learn through impact and repetition, and learning to drive is a great example of repetition. On a conscious level, you are learning to drive, and each time you practice, you are impressing the motions and behaviours of driving into your subconscious mind. Eventually, when you come to a red light, you don't have to stop and think about it. You just step on the brake... automatically. Habits have been formed.

When we find ourselves in an environment where we are required to drive on the opposite side of the road from what we're used to, we have to pay a tremendous amount of conscious attention to what we're doing. Apparently, Phil was driving on the wrong side and, as a result, was involved in a head-on collision. He died instantly. His wife was severely injured and airlifted to the mainland. The kids were shaken up but not physically hurt. If I had asked him on the boat how much longer he thought he had to live, I suspect he would have said at minimum 40 years. As it turned out, he didn't have 40 hours.

The only time you and I have for certain is this very moment. None of us know how many days we have left on this planet. What a shame it would be to trade the only time we know we have – this moment – focusing on something that has happened in the past. On something we cannot change. And worse still, the practice of holding onto guilt and resentment is a good recipe to create more of the same. The subconscious mind doesn't know the difference between past and present. When you are reliving those past injustices, you are soaking up that negative vibration as if it's happening now... all over again... and again... and again... Each time you replay it in your mind, it happens again. And with each replay, the guilt or resentment often grows as if it's being fed (because it is).

If you experience this, as so many of us do, then perhaps it's time for a new freedom statement. "I am so happy and grateful now that I am living in the present. I am moving forward with confidence and a positive expectancy." There has been boatloads of content written about rituals and practices that make the release process more effective. If this is an issue for you, I encourage you to seek out this material.

Let us not look back in anger,
nor forward in fear, but around us in awareness.
**Leland Val Van De Wall, Author, Speaker, Friend &
Mentor to Bob Proctor (and to Joan Posivy)**

I remember quite vividly a woman in one of my Glasgow seminars telling me about an evening that found her once again curled up in a chair in front of the fire, crying over her divorce. Her eight-year old son couldn't bear to see his mom have this experience for even one more night; he went into her bedroom, opened her jewellery box, and took out her wedding ring. He then returned to the living room, marched right past her, and threw the ring into the fire. "Mom," he told her, "it's time for you to let go." We change through impact and repetition. Thanks to her son's impactful actions, this woman got the message and moved on.

Nothing good can come from harbouring resentment or guilt. Learn what you can from it, and move on.

THAT WAS YESTERDAY

I asked Keith and Jeannie Harris how their sweet son Tim – the restaurateur who instinctively loves and trusts everyone at first blush – deals with a situation when things don't go his way. "He's really good at just shrugging it off," Keith explained to me. "He allows himself a window to grieve, so he may grieve in copious amounts for some period of time, and then he says, 'Okay, I'm done.'"

I was intrigued when I heard the story of how they dropped him off at his university residence for the first time. He had never been on his own before. "As soon as they left, I cried and I went to my room," Tim told me. "I cried and I cried and I cried. But then I decided to knock it off and go meet some people."

"When those things become clear to him, he simply moves on," added Keith.

I suggested to Tim's parents that Tim might be much better at letting go of things than they were. They laughed and agreed wholeheartedly. "He cares very deeply, he feels it very strongly, and he'll express it when he needs to," said Jeannie. "But then he really is ready to move on."

During his first year in college, Tim met James, and the two would become incredibly good friends. They were truly inseparable. After first year, though, it turned out that James was not coming back to the college, and he lived in another state. On the last day of school, the two friends were sobbing in each other's arms, and Keith and Jeannie were desperately trying to figure out how to make the transition easier. They even considered buying a plane ticket so Tim could go right away to visit his friend. The next morning at breakfast, though, Keith had an interesting interaction with his son.

"Have you called James?" he asked.

Tim looked up, confused. "Why would I call James?" he replied. "He's not here."

Keith was flabbergasted. "But you were so sad yesterday!" he exclaimed.

"Yes," Tim offered. "I was." Period.

Note the past tense. That was yesterday, today is today. It's time to move on. "Unlike me," Keith observed, "Tim has the ability to let that go and shift gears in some way."

In speaking with Tim, it becomes immediately apparent that he lives entirely in the moment. "People like me, who are students of life… we sometimes go to this place on a mountaintop to try and seek that wisdom of being in the moment," Keith shared with me. "Then it occurred to me, I was going to the wrong mountaintop. I just needed to hang around Tim and watch how it's done. The lessons are right here in our restaurant down the street. All you have to do is go see."

I suggested they should write a book… *Lessons from Tim*. Turns out, it's in the works. Not surprising. Sounds like many of us could use a trip to Tim's Place.

YOUR MAGNIFICENT FUTURE AWAITS

I thought I had this living in the moment thing pretty much under control, until I read *The Power of Now*, by Eckhart Tolle. Through those words, I came to realize pretty quickly how little time I was actually spending in the now. I wanted to change that. My solution? Join a martial arts class!

When there's someone running *at* you whose task it is to take you down, you're not thinking about that person who cut you off in traffic or what you're going to make for dinner. If you do, you go down – fast. You learn very quickly the benefit of being truly present.

I'm so very glad it was Aikido I chose, a Japanese martial art that I've always felt drawn to. When I first stepped into the dojo 10 years ago, I had no idea what I was getting myself into. It was actually five years previous that I had first witnessed the practice at a local demonstration. Rather than sign up then, though, I ran. Fast. I just *could not* see myself doing what they were doing. In my mind, the gap between what I was capable of, with zero experience, and the movements the Aikidoka were performing was just too huge. Years later, when I saw a poster at my local gym, something about it drew me back to the dojo… this time to stay. Tens of thousands of forward rolls, back falls, many trips to Japan to study, and a couple of black belts later, and I still feel very much the beginner.

At a glance, Aikido looks like a bunch of people throwing each other around, falling and rolling at high speed. But in reality, what you see visually on the mat is just a small window into the greater energetic forces at play… just like life itself. What we experience through our sensory factors of sight, smell, sound, taste and touch is merely a physical manifestation of universal energy working behind the scenes, or, more accurately, with and through us. It is this study of energy that really attracted me to the practice of Aikido.. *Ai* can be translated as harmony, or being in harmony with, and *Ki* refers to universal energy or spirit. *Do* in Japanese is similar to the Chinese word *tao*… a way or path of understanding. Aikido, then, is generally translated to mean: *the way of being one (or in harmony) with the universe itself.*

Soon enough, I realized that this path – this way of understanding

— had been calling me in its various renditions for my whole life. Just like my work off the mat, Aikido forces you over and over again to examine the inner workings of the way you think — your beliefs, goals, inspirations and intentions, and the paradigms in which they're rooted. You must discard negative self-talk and limiting beliefs. You must let go of perceived past injustices and focus instead on the moment, right now. You must stay centred, grounded, and steady, and keep your goal clearly in mind. If you don't, you fall. Someone takes you down. But if you do, your practice improves. You get stronger. You can face more skilled and experienced Aikidoka. And as you do, almost without realizing it, you become one yourself. What is your way? Your path? In deepening your understanding of the way of the universe, are you beginning to see how you have the power to choose? Stop waiting. Start doing. It's time for you to begin truly creating the life — the way — that you desire and deserve. It's time to begin.

ACT THREE

BEGIN

> Give yourself the gift of a long-term almost unattainable goal. The beauty of it is, it will shape your life in a direction that you naturally love.
>
> **Chris Hadfield, retired astronaut and Commander of the International Space Station**

I've been saying to you all along that you can have, do, or be anything you believe you can. But you MUST take action, and though beginning anything can be the most difficult step, it is in fact the most vital. It's a key component in *the way success works*.

Consider this. "A rocket travelling from the surface of the Earth to Earth orbit is one of the most energy intensive steps of going anywhere," according to NASA. "*This first step* requires *half* of the total energy needed to go to the surface of Mars."

What that means, in real numbers, is that it takes *the same amount of fuel* to travel the first 400 kilometres of the journey to Earth orbit as it does to travel the next 225,300,000 kilometres to Mars! It takes a *tremendous* amount of power to break away from the Earth's gravitational pull. Similarly, it takes a *huge* amount of effort to discard the constraints of our existing habit patterns and embark on a new journey of goal-achieving activities. It truly is the *starting* that stops most people. But once you make the commitment to yourself that you will achieve certain things, and decide that there's no turning back, things will start to happen and you'll gain momentum, but it may take a tremendous amount of your own inner fuel to overcome inertia. So how do you do it? How do you get the ball rolling and keep it travelling in the right direction? Read on.

CHAPTER EIGHT

GET BY WITH A LITTLE HELP FROM YOUR FRIENDS

It's not just a Beatles lyric. It's the truth. Though you possess more incredible capacity than you can imagine to do whatever it is you dream of, the way is paved by people around you who support, teach, and guide you.

EXPERIENCED MENTORS: NOT OPTIONAL!

All of us need help and support along the way while we are pursuing our goals. Not surprisingly, *every* youth in this book has been helped along by a variety of people – their teachers, colleagues, friends, and mentors. Sometimes, we are even heavily influenced by people we've never met, as was the case with Cameron Johnson (who, as you recall, launched a very profitable business as a pre-teen by selling his sister's Beanie Baby collection). "A mentor does not have to be someone that you meet with for coffee once a week," he says. "I actually have not had that as much as I've had mentors that I know or don't know that I've just studied and read about through their books." He means people like Donald Trump, Michael Dell, and Richard Branson, and admits he was making choices as a result of their influence long before he actually met any of them. "Mentors are crucial," he insists. "Otherwise, you're going through life without a map. The shortest path to success is having a mentor. You can learn so much from them."

Sometimes we just cross our fingers, pick up the phone, and hope that the person we're reaching out to is generous and willing to share their knowledge and experiences to help us along. Such was the case when Nick Waggoner took the leap and called the legendary, incredibly talented ski filmmaker and cinematographer Bill Heath. "We were four college freshmen sitting at the Telluride Mountain Film Festival when we saw Bill Heath's movie *Sinners*," he recalls. "Within a week, we had hatched a plan to drive one of our parents' cars up to Bill's hometown for winter break." He credits Bill for inspiring him to become a filmmaker. "Watching that film was the beginning of our relationship with taking a little camera with us on our trips," says Nick, and it prompted the creation of their first movie, *Handcut*.

Over the years, a heart-warming connection has developed between them. "I have such deep praise for his work," he admits. "Bill has always been a big source of inspiration for me and continues to be. About four months ago, I got this amazing message from his daughter after we released *Valhalla*. 'Your work is such an inspiration to me,' she said. It was so cool continuing the cycle of inspiration and passing it through the generations. Bill inspired me, and I was able to inspire his daughter."

Bill has played a similar role for many people in the industry. His top tip for approaching a potential mentor? "Find out as much as you can about the person's work," he says. "It shows a lot of respect." If they are a filmmaker, watch and study all their movies, read the reviews and the related materials. If they are an author, read all their books. If they run a business, find out all you can about their company. Read their year-end report if it's public, and learn about what's happening in their industry that would be pertinent information once you do get the opportunity to connect with them. You get the picture – it's wise to do your homework. But once you do, take the leap. "Just have the courage to ask," Bill insists.

There is a caution here. When you seek out someone for their advice, make sure you *know* they are getting the results that you want. It sounds so basic, but it's too often missed. Don't ask just anyone!

If you want to become financially independent, for example, don't ask your beer buddy for advice unless he (or she) happens to already be in that position. They might be a great friend, and highly skilled in one (or even many) other areas of their life, but if they're living paycheque to paycheque, they can't possibly tell you how to be financially free. A person can't give you what they don't have. And keep in mind that no one has mastered every area of living – at least not anyone that I know. So you may very likely end up having multiple mentors for different areas of your life.

Back when I first started researching wealthy people and their finances, I learned about something called *passive income*. Back in my banking days, I knew how to generate income only one way – by working. This is what I call *active income*. That means being employed in a job where you're paid by the hour or on a salary. The problem with that is that if we lose our job or are no longer able to do it (or want to do it), we're out of luck. Our one and only source of money is gone. Wealthy people, though, have multiple sources of income, many of which are passive. While they may require a lot of work at the front end to get established, once they are up and running, these income sources require less of your involvement day to day. These include such things as investment income, real estate rental income, royalties and other passive income businesses; think automated car washes, parking lots, or self-storage facilities, for example.

Self-storage facilities in particular began to intrigue me some years ago, and around the same time I encountered a man by the name of Gord Allan who had multiple, multiple sources of income and owned many storage facilities in a number of cities. Gord is definitely someone who knows the industry and, as it turned out, he was willing to be a mentor to me. That first encounter was the law of attraction in action!

During our initial meeting, we discussed the type of information I needed to find and the calculations I needed to consider when contemplating this sort of business. We then set up a date for our next meeting. I'll always remember the first thing he said to me at that next meeting. "What have you done? What did you find out?" he wanted to know. No small talk here. I learned in that moment that Gord was (and is) generous in giving his time and expertise, but he is NOT someone whose time you can waste. He expects results, not excuses.

In the end, my business partner and I *did* get involved in the storage industry, and I'll be forever grateful for Gord's teachings, guidance, and willingness to freely share his knowledge and contacts. Without him, I'm quite sure I couldn't have achieved nearly the successes I have to date. That was 13 years ago, and I'm still involved in the business. And here's a tip for you: there's a national association and regular conferences for just about every industry you can think of – even storage. Yes, I've been to a number of self-storage conferences! During my first one, I met a man who had not yet built or bought a self-storage facility. He came to the conference to find out more about the industry before making a final decision.

And that's a brilliant idea! A good conference offers an enormous variety of resources under one roof. If you're interested in a particular industry, go find one! You can gather all types of valuable information and make contacts with people who are already doing what you want to do. Who knows... you might even meet your next mentor!

IF YOU DON'T ASK, YOU'LL NEVER KNOW

Zachary Rook (break-dancer turned storage and moving man) had a mentor in mind: Tom Potter, leading Australian business superstar. Tom founded his pizza business with one store in 1987, and when he sold the business in 2007, it had grown to more than 250 outlets in Australia and New Zealand with annual sales of $170 million.

"I'm going to go and meet Tom Potter today," declared Zachary one day to a friend. "And he's going to mentor me."

"Yeah, right," she snickered. "He's an untouchable guy. How are you going to do that?"

But Zachary had a plan – mostly. "I figured out where his office was and just waited out front. I had this ignorant persistence about me that he was going to be there and that I was going to meet him."

After three hours of waiting, he finally spotted Tom. He had a chance and took it. He approached the businessman and made a blunt statement. "You need to mentor me," he declared. It wasn't a question, but a statement.

"Okay," Tom replied, "I'm in a hurry. Here's my number." He and Zachary have been friends ever since.

Tom could have said no. There's no guarantee you'll always receive a yes. A person could say no for a whole host of reasons unknown to you that have nothing to do with you. What's important is what *you* say to you. If you get a no, say NEXT! Find another mentor, or ask that same person later on down the road when circumstances have changed. And know that if you do the work of living a meaningful, prosperous, fulfilling life, chances are that one day in the future someone will seek *you* out as a mentor. Full circle.

Perhaps rooted in that experience, Zachary feels strongly about mentoring and has a real desire to give back when and where he can; he became the EO (Entrepreneur's Organization) Brisbane Mentoring Chair for 2014/2015.

Over the years, Fraser Doherty of SuperJam has been helped along by a number of expert mentors too. "I think it's important to be willing to ask for help in the first place," he says. "Many people don't even try asking people they respect for some advice. I found that if I just asked people, often they would be happy to meet me for a coffee. It's important not to expect too much of someone's time – perhaps they'll give you 20 minutes. So figure out what you can ask them that will be most helpful to you. Be specific about what challenges you are facing, and always ask how they actually did what they did."

And Cameron Johnson has a great tip to share. "Always follow up with a thank you note!"

ACCOUNTABILITY PARTNERS

Someone who holds you to your word is an essential component of your goal-achieving repertoire. He or she – your accountability partner – is someone who has agreed to keep you accountable for doing what you've said you're going to do. Ideally, this person is someone for whom you have a deep respect and appreciation so that following through on what you promised to accomplish is simply the only option.

Dave Douglas, author of *Leading the Way*, has been such a person for me. Dave has a vision for his life; he's a goal setter *and* a goal achiever. We meet for lunch a few times a year, and we always walk away from those conversations feeling inspired and motivated; we exchange ideas and do lots of positive brainstorming. Because of his decades of experience working with youth and his passion and commitment for making a difference in their lives, Dave was my first choice of accountability partner when I made a firm decision to launch the Global Youth Project. When I brought it up, he was immediately on board. Since my request was in harmony with his own goals and vision, there was no hesitation in his answer. Everyone needs a Dave in their life, and I'm so thankful to have him in mine!

Every other Monday for the next many, many months, I sent Dave a list of my successes and commitments with dates attached. It was a recap of what I had accomplished in the past two weeks and what I was committed to doing in the next two. Needless to say, there was more than one week that saw me working into the wee hours of the morning to make sure I kept my word.

STRENGTH IN NUMBERS: YOUR MASTERMIND ALLIANCES

"A mastermind alliance," wrote Napoleon Hill, "is built of two or more minds working actively together in perfect harmony toward a common definite object." Other highly-prized people in your life could play this role.

While these alliances tend to encompass four to six people, one of my favourites was a partnership I had with only one other person – Jan Pedersen. She was a communications expert who, like myself, travelled extensively throughout North America and into the United Kingdom as a trainer and seminar leader. Because she was a fellow road-warrior who understood the lifestyle, we were often on the same page. We could really brainstorm well as a team.

Sometimes these partners live in your area, and you can meet them on a regular basis face-to-face. Jan and I didn't have that luxury. We lived in different countries, and this was before Skype and FaceTime! Every Monday morning at the same time, we would meet for 30 minutes by phone. You can accomplish a shocking amount in a half-hour when your meeting is laser-focused.

This is *not* the time to discuss the latest movie or your favourite restaurant! Instead, you each take a brief time to share what good has happened since the last meeting. Then, one person shares something they'd like help with, and a brainstorming session begins to address this issue. Each person has their turn to present their issue to the group and get feedback. Now you see why it's generally limited to four to six people. Stay on time. To wrap up, each person commits to something that they will do as a result of what was discussed.

It was largely because of this mastermind alliance with Jan that I managed to stay on track to release an audio program that came to be known as *No Limit Confidence*. At that time – in addition to all my work on the road – I was also building a house; I know that without my commitment to Jan, my mastermind and accountability partner, it would have been just as easy to put that project off again and again and again. Just like Dilbert the cartoon character, perhaps. "I love deadlines," he jokes. "I particularly love the whooshing sound they make as they go flying by."

Filmmaker Nick Waggoner has developed these sort of alliances from many sources, not the least of which is the team at Sweetgrass Productions. "When I look back over the years, I see a lot of support from my crew and my friends," he says. "That's *so* important to me, and I've learned so much via those relationships. It's beyond words. It's very much a family of people who are working in tandem together."

This also includes celebrating together and accepting awards together, like when they were nominated for the 14th Annual *Powder Magazine* Movie of the Year Award for their film *Valhalla* (described by the team themselves as the tale of one man's search to rediscover the freedom of his youth). Though their beautiful film is more than 60 minutes in length, there are three or so minutes in particular that made the rounds in social media – three minutes where 20 brave skiers carve some sweet runs totally naked. Well, not totally naked. They have skis and boots and helmets and goggles.

When the team got word of their nomination, Nick was ecstatic. "If we win," he suggested, "we'll need to go up there naked. We'll need to accept this award naked."

"There's no way I'm doing that, man," replied Ben, co-director of the film.

But they won. And he did. Everyone was there, including their family and friends, of course, but no one knew what the gang from Sweetgrass had planned for their acceptance speech. "Everybody cheered, and it was this awesome moment," Nick recalls. "To go from that feeling of being these extreme underdogs in the industry and being like this small little niche boutique company to gaining the award and the respect of the people that *we* respect so deeply, it was… an incredible moment."

CHAPTER NINE

THE UNIVERSE ONLY KNOWS HOW TO SAY YES

*When things start to happen it may at first scare you,
and when it stops scaring you, it will never cease to amaze you.*
Bob Proctor

When things start to *really* happen for you, you'll be amazed. When I bought the deli, I was working for a Canadian bank. I shared with a senior staff member my plan to buy the business, and he quickly pointed out why it was a bad idea. He went on to explain the many reasons he felt it would not succeed. Eight months later, when the deli was not only turning a profit but able to support me as well, I quit the bank. "You are so lucky to be able to leave this place," he said. Yes, he *really* said that.

I could have talked to him about how I had to work hard, take calculated risks, put a lot on the line, build and hold an image of what the deli could be, and force myself to stay dancing in the panic zone when all I wanted to do was run – but I didn't. Instead, I just smiled and walked away. I don't believe in luck. I believe in law: the universal law. Know that you can count on the laws to work every time, everywhere, for every person. Period.

Imagine you have before you a fertile plot of land, and in it you plant two seeds — one is poison ivy, and the other is basil. You water and care for them both. In a relatively short period of time, you have two maturing plants. One is poisonous and causes itching, irritation, and sometimes a painful rash; the other is fragrant and versatile and welcomed in many kitchens around the world. The laws of the universe are neither judgmental nor parental. Just like rich, healthy soil, the universe will accept any seed you give it and support its growth. If you give a lot of time, energy, and attention to negative circumstances — if you nurture and care for those seeds — you are unknowingly creating more of the same. *Don't do that!*

Instead, build an image on the screen of your mind of the life and the person you want to become, and immerse yourself in that picture however you can. Plant *that* seed. Let *that* image be the root of your decision-making and your guiding light — not your present circumstances.

> **Two of the most precious and powerful times to do your visualization work are before you fall asleep at night and just after you wake in the morning.**

EMPOWERED EVENINGS

If you tend to fall asleep to the doom and gloom of TV or online news coverage… stop. At best, you're opening the door to a host of physical and mental health problems that have been linked to that nighttime practice; at worst, you're layering onto that a range of negative inputs to your psyche. Just like your heart is still beating and your blood is still pumping, your subconscious is still rolling onward while your conscious mind takes a break.

On the headboard of my bed is a little sign. "Good things are happening," it reads. I love it! It's such a beautiful affirmation to fall asleep with. "I beseech you to go into your sleep mode by using your mind to assume the feeling of your wishes being fulfilled," suggests Dr. Wayne Dyer. "This is the beginning of a reprogramming of your subconscious mind."

Before falling asleep, give thanks for everything that happened in the day for which you are grateful; notice how comforting this can be. As you are reflecting on the events of the day, consider anything you did or said that wasn't in harmony with the new you (with your freedom statement). Rather than putting yourself down about it, relive that scenario in your mind's eye as you would have liked it to be. Perhaps it was an encounter with someone that didn't go the way you would have liked or maybe a conversation among friends where your words just wouldn't flow, and you struggled to get your point across. See yourself instead speaking calmly, eloquently, and with perfect confidence. Relive that a couple of times with feeling. It will help you be better prepared for next time as you're nurturing the seed of what you *do* want versus what you don't – the old paradigm. Think of it as peak performance training that you do as if you were a top athlete. You visualize your performance and the corresponding desired outcome. Winning athletes don't play and replay in their minds what went wrong – their coaches train them to visualize a *perfect* performance. When you do this with intention, with true feeling and a strong emotional connection, the subconscious mind can't tell the difference between what's real and what's imagined. So decide on something, believe it, and then do it!

THE HUG SEEN AROUND THE WORLD

Until we get to the point where we can conceive of something we would like to have, do, or be and instantly put ourselves in that vibration of belief (and stay there!), we need to utilize tools like freedom statements and visions boards and daily doses of the right ideas. Trusting, loving, and remarkably able to let go of the past in the blink of an eye, Tim Harris has yet another remarkable ability... once he decides on something – he believes it. End of discussion!

In 2014, Tim and his parents were invited to the White House for a formal state dinner, which was held as a tribute to Special Olympics competitors – many of whom were also present. Tim has been involved with the Special Olympics since he was just 13 years old, and he has an enormous collection of medals from competing in basketball, hockey, volleyball, golf, and track and field. (He told me he has more gold medals than Michael Phelps.)

During the dinner, President Obama was sharing a bit about each of the athletes in attendance that evening. His comments about Tim included a reference to his restaurant as well as all the sports in which he competes.

"The most popular item is the hug Tim gives his customers," he read aloud. And then he looked out at the audience, searching for Tim. "I didn't get a hug!" he exclaimed. "Come on, man."

That's all Tim needed to hear. He leaped out of his seat, ran to the stage, and delivered a much applauded presidential hug. "I love you, Obama," he said to the president.

"I love you back!" said Obama. "Presidents need some encouragement once in a while too. That felt really good. That was nice. Thank you, Tim."

"It was the hug seen around the world," says Keith, Tim's dad, about that day in Washington. "The photo of it was in newspapers in 30 countries. It was a magical moment."

Now here's the real lesson for us all.

Tim and his family found out less than a week prior to the event that they were invited. When the manager of Tim's restaurant heard the news, he was ecstatic. "Oh my gosh, Tim," he said, "you get to shake the hand of the president!"

"I'm not going to shake his hand," Tim laughed. "I'm going to give the president a hug!"

Jeannie, Keith, and the manager tried to explain that you can't just run up and hug the president of the United States. "But what did we know?" Jeannie admits. "Tim knew. He just doesn't doubt."

"We think too much," Keith adds. "Tim starts with a belief, not a series of thoughts that become a belief. He does this amazing shortcut. He goes straight to it."

In you ever find yourself in Albuquerque, New Mexico, and feel like you could use a hug, stop in at Tim's Place Restaurant. You'll find that ***a hug*** is on the menu. I'm told that for Tim, that was a non-negotiable item in the business plan. He has a pocket counter via which he keeps track of the number of hugs he's given out in a day. His tally is then added to the electronic hug counter on the wall of the restaurant. At time of writing, Tim had given out over 70,000 of them!

MINDFUL MORNINGS

As I'm waking up, I'll record any idea or inspiration that comes to mind. Afterwards, when I'm up out of bed, I'll play my pre-recorded audio and internalize the words I hear while looking at my vision board. It's a phenomenal way to start the day. And just like the evening routine, it's very quick – 10 minutes at the most. But the reward is huge. You're starting your day not only on the right foot but in the right vibration.

Remember I pointed out that a habit is something you do automatically, without giving it any conscious thought? You have a series of morning habits that likely include brushing your teeth, washing your face, getting dressed, checking your email... Aside from your email, those things are all related to the health of your body and hygiene. What do you do for the health of your mind?

In addition to your mindful morning work, it's vitally important that you invest a relatively short period of time each day in your personal development. It seems that the majority of us were not raised to understand the importance of this, but your results in life are determined by... you. So the more you can improve your effectiveness, the more options and opportunities you will have. Choose action over reaction.

I once ran a series called *Learning Luncheons* where I would teach a success principle, and then we'd have a group discussion on how we could apply the principle to our business and personal lives. Warren, one of the first people who signed up for the series, owned a successful office equipment business in the town. When he showed up for the first luncheon, someone recognized him. "Why are you here?" they asked. "You don't need this!"

"This stuff works," he pointed out. "That's why I keep coming back." Warren understood that personal development isn't a one-shot deal. It's a lifelong practice.

CHAPTER TEN

CULTIVATE HABITS OF SUCCESS

YOUR HIGHEST ROI: CONTINUAL SELF-IMPROVEMENT

(Yes that's right. ROI = Return on Investment.) Do you feel as though you always have a problem to deal with? That there's always something to fix, deal with, get done or solve? Truth be told, there will always be obstacles, issues, problems... life is full of them. Often people hope that something will change in their life so they'll no longer have any problems at all. They feel that something – maybe the right partner, or a better job, or more money – will solve everything. But the something that needs to change, of course, is within themselves.

It's not that our problems go away as we get better at standing in our own power and building these personal development skills. As we grow as a person, though, we become more effective at handling problems. They don't necessarily disappear, but our capacity and ability to deal with them improves as we build on the rest of these skills.

People like Tim Cook, CEO of Apple, Inc. and Mary Barra, CEO of General Motors, for example, have become extremely skilled at handling problems, and they are compensated well for it. They manage hundreds of thousands of employees worldwide. As you and I form the daily habit of engaging in personal development work, our stock goes up too.

There are so many excellent resources available to us at the click of a mouse or a swipe of the screen; all we need to do is choose which area we want to focus on next – developing our sales skills, dealing with stress, finessing negotiation strategies, leading a team, improving communication practices... These are examples of *soft skills*. Hard skills come from technical training – product knowledge and computer skills, for example.

In the *Forbes* article "The 10 Skills Employers Most Want in 2015 Graduates," writer Susan Adams identifies the top three attributes employers want in new hires: the ability to work in a team structure, the ability to make decisions and solve problems, and the ability to communicate verbally with people inside and outside an organization. All soft skills. The hard skills of technical knowledge and proficiency with computer software programs didn't hit the list until #7 and #8.

I've worked with and provided training for thousands of managers over the years, and without question, the soft skills are *much* more difficult to teach. In my hiring experience, I'll always choose a great attitude and minimum hard skills over boatloads of knowledge and a challenging temperament. A person with a great attitude is often very teachable and eager to learn; they'll typically seek out the technical skills they need as they need them.

Google, it seems, thinks along these same lines. For the February 2014 *New York Times* article "How to Get a Job at Google," writer Thomas L. Friedman interviewed Laszlo Bock, the Senior VP of People Operations at the tech behemoth. "The world only cares about – and pays off on – what you can do with what you know (and it doesn't care how you learned it). And in an age when innovation is increasingly a group endeavour, it also cares about a lot of soft skills – leadership, humility, collaboration, adaptability and loving to learn and relearn. This will be true no matter where you go to work." The least important of the attributes Google looks for, according to Bock, is expertise. Of course, if it's a technical role they are hiring for, they will assess your coding ability, he points out, but for *every job* the number one thing they look for is learning ability.

Time and time again, when I ask an audience full of managers to think about a top performer in their organization and consider what makes them a star, the attributes they share are always soft skills. This learning about yourself and improving your soft skills doesn't need to take a lot time each day… as long as you do a little bit each day. Part of my morning fitness routine involves a series of stretches that can take 30 to 60 minutes, depending on my schedule. This is my time to have a useful audiobook, video teaching, or podcast playing. Your vehicle or public transit can serve the same function as you make your way to work or play – consider it a learning centre on wheels. Turning your travel time into your learning time is a wise investment in yourself, and is guaranteed to pay rich dividends.

THE HUMAN ELEMENT

When Zachary Rook was piecing together his business after the flood, his involvement with the Entrepreneur's Organization was key. One of the primary lessons he stumbled across during that process is one that holds true for all of us who do any sort of work – self-employed or not. "Within the forum at EO," he explains, "they're not mentors; you're all peers, even if someone's got a $100 million business, and you've got a $1 million business. So one of the most remarkable things I realized is that no matter what your business is, 90% of it is the same. Someone can be running an IT business or farm, but so many of your issues are identical. And so many of those issues are human-based."

I've always said that regardless of who writes your cheque each week, ultimately, you're self-employed. And developing your ability to deal with others will pay great dividends in every area of your life.

Cameron Johnson has learned how to deal effectively with others. He's proven his success over and over at managing people online in collaborative virtual environments and live in brick-and-mortar facilities like the 100-employee dealership opened by his grandfather in 1937. "For me, it's always about the challenge," he says. "Even when I've grown our dealership over the last five years, I still wanted another challenge. That challenge was to go buy another dealership that was the worst in the state of Virginia – a total mess that was failing and was losing about $400,000 annually." At the time of writing, that failing dealership was in its second month under Cameron's wing and already turning a profit.

But the important point here is that he's quick to identify that the success of the new dealership was entirely a team effort. "Some of the managers in my team have been with our business for 20 years, and things have always been fairly consistent. They've always just come in and done their job at our main dealership. When I was able to spring it on them, they were all energized. They put so much time and energy into making it work. It wasn't me... it was my whole team. They just really rose to the occasion. They made it happen a lot faster than I would have expected."

But in my experience, his team would not have rallied to the cause and made that new dealership such a success had it not been for Cameron's ability to lead... his soft skills.

MAKING QUANTUM LEAPS IN YOUR PRODUCTIVITY

1. Manage activities, not time.

As much as we sometimes think we'd like to, we can't manage time. Regardless of who we are or where we live, there are 1,440 minutes in every day. (It sounds like more when you say it in minutes.) Both the most productive, goal-achieving person in the world and any person who doesn't do much at all are gifted with exactly the same amount. It's how you approach those minutes that will determine how much you can get done in a day without overloading or overwhelming yourself.

There are many great tips and techniques that can help you sort this out, but when it comes to organizing your time, it really comes down prioritizing. The ability to decipher what's important *and then work accordingly* is a must. We've all had days where we've started out thinking we'll be incredibly productive, and before you know it you are bowled over by interruptions, emergencies, and a whole host of got-to-deal-with-this-now-type situations. Knowing what your priorities are will help guide your decision-making throughout the day and avoid sheer chaos!

2. From big picture to small task.

So what *is* your criteria for prioritizing? It *should* be based on the long-term vision on your life. What's the big picture you're working toward? If you don't know, taking the time to figure that out and define it will pay huge dividends for you in increased productivity and effective decision-making (which actually means getting a lot more accomplished and having way more fun). That grand vision is your compass. As opportunities arise or decisions need to be made, you simply need to determine if their offerings are in alignment with your bigger picture. Does it lead me in the right direction? Or guide me astray?

Will you change your vision in the future? Very likely, yes. What was important to you in a previous decade might be quite different today. As you learn more about your true self and the capabilities you possess (as well as the intricacies of the outside world), your vision of what you can accomplish in this lifetime will expand.

So how is your big vision realized? Essentially, through the accomplishment of your major goals. And to accomplish the big ones, you first need to achieve your many smaller ones – the ones that are the result of your daily activities. It's all connected. This is the link. This is how what you're doing today – no matter how small and insignificant is seems on a grander scale – is actually the foundation of your larger vision. Consider Andy-Stuart Hill, whose vision (his big picture) was to be a true world traveller… not just a tourist, but someone who really connects with the local people in all the countries he visits. An example of a major goal, for him, was a recent expedition to the South Pole; smaller goals which led to that were securing funding and attaining a certain level of fitness to make the trek. Logically, then, his daily choices were based in part on incorporating exercise, eating healthy and nourishing foods, and carefully following his budget.

The reality is that we can't manage time, only activities. And this is where your discipline comes in – in doing what you know needs to be done.

Bob Proctor gives the best definition I've heard. "Discipline is giving yourself a command," he says, "and then following it." Write down what you know needs to be done….*and then do it*. Whether or not you give the command will make the difference between accomplishing a little or a lot!

3. The vital few: is this an 80 or a 20?

Joseph Juran, a pioneer in the field of quality management, developed what became known as the Pareto Principle, or the 80/20 rule. It calls to our attention where we are spending most of our time – on the **vital few** important things or the **trivial many**.

As this concept is well-known in management circles, it's an excellent example of knowing versus doing. Many of us have heard of this idea, but too few really follow through on making use of it! If you do integrate this principle into your daily task management, then congratulations… you and I both know you're already a goal achiever! If it's not, consider this observation:

80% of the value coming out of an entire set comes from 20% of the items. The other 80% of the items, although they take a great deal of time, energy, and resources, nevertheless account for only 20% of the total value coming out of the same set.

For example:
* *20% of the streets in a city handle 80% of the traffic.*
* *20% of a product's features get used 80% of the time. (Think smart phone apps, computer software, etc.)*

Businesses use the rule to increase profitability because they've realized:
* *80% of company sales come from 20% of the sales staff.*
* *80% of company profit comes from 20% of staff activities.*
* *80% of the problems come from 20% of the staff.*

Clearly, these values lack statistical precision, but what the rule provides is an impetus for us to look at where we spend our time and our resources *today* and correct our trajectory as needed. Unfortunately, most people fail to set priorities based on their goals and, consequently, spend the majority of their time on minor, unimportant, seemingly urgent tasks. The result? They achieve far less than they could if they re-assessed. There is no question that highly effective people consistently focus their attention on the vital few tasks and avoid the trivial many.

Essentially, you need to look at what you do in a day. Chances are, only a small percentage (20%?) of the tasks you perform will be providing results in the direction you want to go. Identify those, and figure out how to spend more time on them to get more and better results. In order to do that, chances are that you'll have to find someone else to handle some of the other current 80%, or eliminate those less helpful tasks all together.

A person can be busy all day and get plenty done, but if they've been working mostly on low-payoff tasks, then they've merely been efficient – not effective.

> Efficiency is doing things right.
> Effectiveness is doing the right things.
> **Peter F. Drucker, Management Consultant**

I imagine you can guess that the right things are in fact the things that lead you toward achieving your goals and ultimately your vision. Keep reminding yourself that what you do today (no matter how small) MUST contribute to your big vision. Otherwise, you're wasting your time.

FAST-TRACK YOUR SUCCESS: WATCH, LEARN & EMULATE

Many of the youth I met in the course of writing this book told me that a key to their success was to ask for advice and guidance from people who were already doing well at what they wanted to do. In my youth, when I was employed in the financial industry, I worked with a very successful man named Consiglio Di Nino. Con, as he was known, began as a teller for a Canadian bank when he was 17. He went on to become co-founder, president, and CEO of the trust company where I eventually became branch manager. He was one of the first people to open my eyes to how much someone could accomplish in a day when they had focus. Over my years there, I picked up a few key lessons from this very busy (and successful) man that are worth emulating.

1. *Work on your priorities.*

Con was a busy guy. Not only did he have his full-time commitments in the financial industry to take care of, he managed an impressive list of volunteer activities in support of community service groups and causes that were near and dear to him. After leaving the financial sector, he went on to become a senator for the government of Canada. In order to fit all those things into his 1,440 minutes every day, Con had to have a very clear list of priorities. Which things needed to get done to support his vision? And which were simply wasting his time? Part of his success surely came from figuring out which was which.

2. *Walk your talk.*

When Con said that his staff was important, he meant it. One day, he and I returned from a luncheon and were greeted in his office by a huge stack of phone messages. I watched as he proceeded to flip through them all and pull out any that were from staff members. Those, he was returning first. Whether he realized it or not, he showed me that day that if I – one of his staff – really needed to speak to him, he'd be there for me. That was reassuring, to say the least.

3. Always do your best.

Con taught me to always be on the lookout for great future staff. Even if you don't need to fill a position immediately, he pointed out, you never know when you'll need someone fabulous, so always be looking for an individual whom you might want to hire. Anytime I'm in a retail store or service facility and receive exemplary service, I make a mental note that they might just be a future employee. On the other side of the coin, if you happen to be working in a place that you feel is short-term or maybe not where you want to be – still give it your absolute best. You never know who might see the way you work and have something great to offer you.

4. Make your life meaningful.

When I made the decision to leave the firm and move out west, Con sent me away with two pieces of advice. The first was to be careful in the mountains – after all, it was a far cry from the streets of Toronto. The second really hit home. "Be sure you make something of your life," he told me. I've never forgotten that. When things seem to get out of control, I step back and consider my list of activities in the context of living a meaningful life – in other words, that advice helps me evaluate if what I'm doing – every moment of every day – is in alignment with my bigger picture. If not, it's out.

APPRECIATION FOR WINNING (AND LOSING)

Back in college, Nick (now of Sweetgrass Productions fame) and his buddies entered a film short into a local festival. It was a composite of a number of scenes they had shot over the years, and the closing shot declared: COMING, FALL 2008.

They had no idea how they were going to make a full-length film. But, by announcing it, they had committed to it. Now there was no backing down.

Nick concedes today that deep down, he must have known they could pull it off; on the surface, though he was experiencing a completely different feeling. "This is a horrible idea, I was thinking. How could it ever work? I felt like a very tiny minnow in a very big pond. It was tough to have anybody give you the time of day or take you seriously."

After reaching out to many companies for sponsorship, Nick was excited to get an email back. "Are you going to be at the OR?" it asked. It sounded to Nick like some kind of event, so he googled it. Sure enough, the potential sponsor was referring to the Outdoor Retailer trade show, held twice a year, which attracts thousands of buyers and senior level decision makers. And it was happening in just 10 days. Not only was this the first he'd heard of it, but Nick was scheduled to board a plane to South America for that semester away from school in just two days!

He didn't hesitate. Instead, he changed his plans. Nick grabbed all his ski gear and hitchhiked across the country to attend this trade show on his way to South America. Did he get the sponsorship he was seeking? Nope. But what he *did* get was valuable experience – experience that paid off six months later when he returned to the market.

This time he didn't have to hitchhike. Nick borrowed a car from a friend and drove more than 1000 km, overnight, in a snowstorm, from Colorado Springs to Salt Lake City. He arrived in the wee hours of the morning and was on the trade show floor by 8 a.m.

"I walked by Patagonia," he recalls, "and I had this moment when I thought, 'I'm not good enough for Patagonia. Why would they ever want to work with us? We're not cool enough. There's no way.'" (A well-known outdoor clothing and supplies company with lofty goals and high-end products, Patagonia is a *big* deal; they showed sales in 2013 of roughly $600-million dollars.) "I hesitated for a second, and then I thought, you know… maybe it *is* worth a shot. Maybe we should go and talk to them. So I sat down and had a meeting with their marketing guy – a total cold call."

Two months later, Nick got an email from Patagonia. He and his team got the sponsorship.

This was, without doubt, a big win. Sometimes though, big losses can be just as potent in contributing to your attainment of that big picture. I recently heard Bob Proctor say he treats the two events the same; you learn immensely from both. Cameron Johnson says something similar. "The really critical point about winning is this: when you don't win, you can't let that get in your way. Winning gives you the confidence and courage you deserve – but it's important to know how to appreciate the opportunities for growth that often come *with just having been in the race*. I believe you can learn more from failure than you can from success. Failing allows you to critique your mistakes, learn from them, and correct them in the future."

"Everything happens for a reason," he adds. "When somebody loses their job, when they get their separation papers, it's the worst day of their life… then all of a sudden, they start seeing doors open and opportunities open, and then, hopefully, things work out. Many people have started a business that they didn't intend on by first losing their job."

Indeed, during seminars when I've talked to people in this situation, many have confided that deep down they had wanted to start their own business but had lacked the confidence to quit their job and pursue it. The universe looked after granting their secret wish. That darn orange seed!

PERSISTENCE

All the youth you've read about here have developed that quality of *persistence* to one degree or another. Otherwise, they wouldn't have such successful stories to tell. Persistence is about picking yourself up and giving it another try. "I don't think I have any particular talent that other people don't have," offers jam entrepreneur Fraser Doherty, "but I guess I am just more willing than most to keep trying when my ideas don't work the first time around. I only do all of this because I think it's fun. When you find it fun, you don't really mind if it works or not. You end up working really hard at it and, chances are, it becomes a success."

When you think you've exhausted all the possibilities, remember this: you haven't.
Robert Schueller, author of
Success Is Never Ending, Failure Is Never Final

More than once when I've reached the point of wanting to give up on solving a particular problem or facing a particular challenge, Schueller's quote would come to mind and cause me to look at the situation anew. "What have I missed?" I'll ask myself. "What am I not seeing?" If the answer *still* doesn't come, perhaps it's time to brainstorm with a friend, mentor, or mastermind partner. I can only filter a situation through my own paradigms and, at times, those filters prevent me from seeing a solution that is starkly obvious to someone else.

Recently this riddle showed up in my inbox. It was an excellent reminder of the limitations of our paradigms and how they trick us into believing that problems are unsolvable.

> *A father and son were once driving in a car on a highway. Unfortunately, the car met with an accident and the father died on the spot. The son was badly injured. He was rushed to the hospital where the city's best surgeon attended on him. The surgeon looked at the boy and said, "I cannot operate on my son." Who was the surgeon?*

Do you know? Before reading down the page too far, read the scenario again. Don't feel bad if you don't come up with an answer. Most people don't. The reason why it's difficult is that most of us have some preconceived notion of who a surgeon might be. An older male, perhaps. But the surgeon, in this case, is the boy's mother.

We may believe that how we see things – our beliefs, perceptions, and thought processes are clear and true and unprejudiced, when in fact we all view the world (and ourselves) through our paradigms, our unique set of assumptions, values and concepts that we know to be our reality. That's why when we feel – or are – stuck, it can be immensely helpful to be challenged in our thinking or approach by a good friend or mentor. Be thankful that these people are in your life and can encourage you to see things in a different light!

GRATITUDE

Another common thread between the youth I interviewed for this book is that they all talked about giving back and making the world a better place. More and more, I see this desire permeating the next generation.

Cameron Johnson sums it up nicely. "True prosperity isn't something you take from the world: it's something you share *with* the world."

"I find that my generation of entrepreneurs is willing to invest a lot of their time and profits in doing good for a particular community," says Fraser Doherty. "Getting rich isn't the most important motivation in their lives. In my case, I take far more satisfaction from an elderly person telling me that our tea parties make them feel like a person again than I could ever take from trying to make lots of money to buy expensive clothes."

The tea parties Fraser refers to are his way of saying thank you to his grandmother's generation. SuperJam has hosted more than a hundred of these tea party events across the UK that feature live music, dancing, and of course, scones and jam. A lot of the people who come out to these events live in care homes or in senior's housing, and an opportunity to meet new friends and have an afternoon out can be quite rare. I asked Fraser about his favourite tea party moment. "A few years ago, we hosted a massive tea party in Edinburgh for about 600 elderly people," he recalls. "It was really exciting to pull off an event of that size – it took a lot of volunteers, and I was *so* happy to see other people joining in with our vision of giving elderly people some fun."

His grandmother is having fun too. Earlier this year, Fraser was awarded an MBE (Member of the Order of the British Empire) by the Queen for services to business. "While I never did any of this to win awards, it is of course an honour when that sort of thing happens," he admits. "And it was a wonderful day out when I took my grandmother to Buckingham Palace to meet Prince Charles!" He did, after all, have her recipe to thank for that.

WHEN TO START? TODAY IS GOOD!

There is simply no substitute for taking action. We can dream and plan and talk about what we'd like to do, but until we make that critical decision that we're going to go for it, our results won't change. By now it should be clear that you don't need to know all the steps required to manifest your goals. You only need to see and take the first step.

> Faith is taking the first step, even when
> you don't see the whole staircase.
> **Dr. Martin Luther King, Jr.**

Know that you don't have to go it alone. You've got to provide the vision, determination, and willingness to take action, *but there will be help* available for you along the way – if you're open to it. Begin. Once you do, you'll be amazed at what shows up in your life to help you take the next step.

CHAPTER ELEVEN

IT'S A WRAP

We've covered a lot of ground since page one. Here is a checklist of the main concepts, ideas, and suggestions that you'll want to be sure to embrace.

DECIDE (ACT I)

This is where it all starts – a decision. What is it that you would like to have, do, or be? This step may sound like a no-brainer to you. It might seem too obvious. But you'd be amazed at the number of people who simply never do this. They get so involved in their day-to-day living that they never take the time to step back and design their life. Consequently, they do less and achieve less than they are capable of.

If you haven't already done so…

* Explore the big picture for your life by answering the **4 Primary Questions (p. 22)**.
* Then fill in the details by creating **Your List of 100** goals **(p. 29)**.

* It's **Decision Time (p. 35)**. Choose the goals you're ready to pursue.
* **Bring Your Goals to Life (p. 37)** by imagining yourself as the person already in possession of them.

Thanks to **universal law**, these steps put you in the vibratory rate of everything (and everyone) that is required for the fulfillment of your picture. You'll recall that everything in the universe is in a constant state of vibration, even those things that appear solid or inert to the naked eye. Everything is either growing or dying, being created or decaying. When the orange seed is planted, its vibratory rate dictates what it will attract. In the ground, the seed is surrounded by particles of energy, but it will only attract those which are harmonious. As it does this, it expands. We call that growth. And the roots and shoots start to develop. The entire tree doesn't instantly appear when the seed is planted. There is a process. Day by day, bit by bit, the orange tree is emerging. The same logic applies for whatever you decide to grow into. Staying *in tune* with the good that you desire is vital.

So how do you stay in the right vibration?

* Create and use your **vision board** and **audio recordings (p. 40)**.

BELIEVE (ACT II)

When you get feeling you can't do something – something that you want with your whole head and whole heart – remember that feeling *is not a reflection of your potential* but rather of your subconscious conditioning expressed through the filter of your paradigms.

* **Put an End to Mental Malpractice (p. 67)**. When you bad mouth yourself, it's like planting a garden full of poison ivy. Your little

aspiring orange sprout won't stand a chance.
* *Create **freedom statements (p. 69)** to describe the person you wish to become. Repeat them often and with integrity.*
* *As you step out in pursuit of your goals, congratulations! **Welcome to the Panic Zone (p. 72)**. Don't run! Re-read the chapter. Again. And again.*
* *Consider **The Company You Keep (p. 79)**. Are the people you spend the most time with positive and productive? If not, you have some decisions to make about who you want to be a part of your amazing life.*
* *Take control of your life by **Taking Control of Your Thinking (p. 96)**.*
* *Never again play the blame game. There is no benefit.*
* *Release all resentments and guilt. No good can come to you from being in the negative state that these emotions evoke.*

BEGIN (ACT III)

No amount of reading or memorizing will make you successful in life. It's the understanding and application of wise thoughts that bring you results!

* *Reach out to your ideal **mentors, accountability partners,** and potential **mastermind members.***
* *Strive to feed your mind with positive, uplifting thoughts, as **The Universe Only Knows How to Say Yes (p. 123)**.*
* *Plan and execute your **Empowered Evenings (p. 124)** and **Mindful Mornings (p. 127)**.*
* *Become addicted to lifelong learning, and engage in **Continual Self-Improvement (p. 129)**.*
* *Tie your daily activities to your goals by **Making Quantum Leaps in Your Productivity (p. 133)**. You'll be so impressed by how much you can accomplish, and you'll be in a better frame of mind doing it.*

People will be amazed at how much you begin to accomplish in your 1,440 minutes a day. Not because you're overworked (a well-balanced set of goals will see to that), but because you've become focused. You're spending time on things that are truly important to you. You'll recall that Cameron Johnson explained how he really wasn't any different from the other kids at school; he just chose to spend his after-school time differently than his buddies.

What do you do with your list as goals *desired* begin to transform into goals *achieved*? Many people tell me of the great sense of satisfaction they receive by crossing things off their lists – and keeping those lists as a nice reminder of how far they've come. But remember too that when things don't go as you've planned, have an **Appreciation for Winning (And Losing) (p. 139)**.

Not only can there be great lessons in failures, which may prove invaluable to you in the future when the stakes are higher, but sometime the loss is exactly what's needed to happen for you to take the next step. As I was writing this final chapter, I heard a clip of Nick Woodman, founder of GoPro, explaining that when he invented his camera, he did not know how to build a business around it, so he went looking for a licensing deal. This way he would simply be paid a royalty. At one point he was in licensing talks with Kodak, but, ultimately, they backed out. "At the time, I was disappointed," he said, "but, boy, was I lucky they didn't licence it because it forced me to go build GoPro!" Today, his company is worth billions.

As you keep your sights on your goals, there may be events that on the surface *appear* to be failures, mistakes, or losses. At worst, they're valuable teaching tools. At best, they could be blessings in disguise!

Finally, foster an attitude of **Gratitude (p. 143)** by being thankful for all the good in your life TODAY *and* for all the good that is coming your way.

CONCLUSION

NOW IS YOUR TIME TO SHINE

Every youth I interviewed for this book is special. And the same can be said about you. Sometimes when we read the stories of other people's accomplishments, we forget to be inspired and revert instead to that pattern of negative self-talk. "Maybe they can do that, but I can't," is a common response to others achieving great things. I hope by this point you have completely, without a doubt, convinced yourself that this is not true. You are every bit as capable of achieving your heart's desire as anyone else.

There really, truly, honestly is no one quite like you. While we all come from the same source, each of us possesses a totally unique blend of talents, abilities, qualities and characteristics unlike anyone else.

And what a perfect time to be on the planet to uncover, expand on, and share our gifts! I feel blessed to be alive in an era where humankind is finally moving from an energy of competition to one of collaboration and creativity. This is not yet expressed by everyone, everywhere… but the shift *is* happening.

Around the globe, youth of all ages are not just *talking* about how to improve the quality of their lives and those people they want to serve, they're doing it – together. You've met some of them in these pages.

You too are now aware that the results you currently see in your life – your happiness, your health, and your wealth – are merely a product of your thinking up until now, and they are in no way a reflection of your true potential. In truth, no one knows what greatness you are capable of – maybe not even you! (Yet!)

Remember Nick Waggoner's observation about his reality being so much more than he could have ever imagined or dreamed of? Your own version of that experience is available to you too. It may not be with a camera. Perhaps it's with a pen, a paintbrush, a computer, your hands, your voice, your body or your intellect, but **whatever is in your heart to pursue, I encourage you to go for it.** You will not yet know all the steps you'll need to take, but that's okay. You know the first one now, and you won't be travelling alone.

Be like a sculptor, chipping away at the negative and limiting beliefs that have been holding you back. As you do, you will come to experience more and more of the glow that is your true self, and your life will never be the same again. You *will* amaze yourself. And the world will be a better place because you're here. Decide. Believe. Begin.

ACKNOWLEDGEMENTS

WITHIN THESE PAGES, I'VE SHARED with you the stories of many of the people who have made a profound difference in my life and therefore have on some level contributed to the book's content and creation. To each of them, I will always be grateful.

I must extend a special note of deep gratitude to my teacher and mentor Bob Proctor who first introduced me to the love of lifelong learning and opened my eyes to the vast study of the mind and human potential so many years ago. It's my ongoing mission to pay it forward.

I am so very thankful to every youth I interviewed for this book who believed in this project and allowed me to share their story. Each of you is truly a shining light for us all. In addition, there are a few others I'd like to introduce to you who have been valuable contributors behind the scenes.

Ayva Cowell. If I were a superhero, Ayva would be my superpower! She has a seemingly bottomless store of talents, not the least of which is her ability to take what I've written and make it come alive in a way that is well beyond my realm of expertise. This book simply would not be what it is without her editorial craftsmanship and keen designer's eye.

Karl Masewich. This, of course, is who encouraged me at the age of 19 to say yes! He's been my friend, confidant, business partner, sounding board, and greatest source of humour and encouragement for 35 years. (Please don't do the math!) I value his presence in my life more than words could say.

Carol-Anne Fisher. A person with a bigger heart you simply could not find. She's been a huge cheerleader of my pursuits all my life, and I'm so very thankful to call her my big sister.

Jean-René Leduc Sensei. My dear friend Jean-René has been my Aikido teacher for a decade. As a 6th degree black belt (having devoted the last 30 years to his study), he is a gifted teacher who has taught me more about universal energy than I could have ever experienced through books – a gift I will always treasure and continue to pursue.

Philipp Gawthrop & Miryam Huchet. Through the art of Aikido, I have been exposed to a network of amazing people around the globe. But it all began with my first teachers, Philipp and Miryam. I'll be forever grateful for their compassion and guidance, both on and off the mats.

Ryan Sutcliffe. Walking and talking with Ryan about the ideas presented in this book has been a treasured mainstay of our relationship for the past 20 years. I am exceptionally thankful for his conversation and friendship.

Jennifer Matosevic and Patrick Sawyer. I am very grateful to these youth, whom I've had the pleasure of working with in the past, for taking the time to read through the manuscript of this book and provide thoughtful commentary and suggestions.

Linda Cole, Ruth Prosser, and Helen Price. By taking care of business back at the office, these women gave me the opportunity and freedom to devote all the time and attention needed to bring this project to fruition. Their support has been a true gift.

Sigrid Macdonald. I feel blessed that this incredibly talented, experienced, and insightful editor was excited to be part of this project. With her involvement, I felt reassured that this project was in good hands.

Peggy McColl. Her immense knowledge of the publishing world caused me to see how this book could be created and then shared with the world.

This last acknowledgement should perhaps be at the top of the list. *It is to you, dear reader.* I feel so very grateful that you chose to bring this book into your life. Thank you. And I wish you the greatest joy and success imaginable in living your best life.

MEET OUR FEATURED YOUTH

It was a real joy to connect with each one of these youthful achievers. I hope you found their stories to be as inspiring and motivating as I have. In alphabetical order by first name:

Cameron Johnson, USA
www.cameronjohnson.com
Entrepreneur, Speaker
Author of *You Call the Shots* ©

Deep Shankar Saha, India
www.facebook.com/deepshankarsaha
President of Rotaract Club of Altruism
www.facebook.com/rco.altruism
Founder of the *VBB: Virtual Blood Bank*

Fraser Doherty, Scotland
www.fraserdoherty.com
Creator of *SuperJam*
Author of *SuperBusiness* ©

Nick Waggoner, USA/Canada
www.sweetgrass-productions.com
Filmmaker, Director & Producer
Sweetgrass Productions

MEET OUR FEATURED YOUTH
(CONTINUED)

Rachel Pautler, Canada
www.suncayr.ca
CEO & Co-founder, *Suncayr*

Tim Harris, USA
www.timsplace.com
Founder, *Tim's Restaurant*
(For Breakfast, Lunch, & Hugs)

Tugi Ryan Togiaheulu, NZ & China
Pablo Sinclair, New Zealand
www.facebook.com/feelgoodhappydays
Founders of *#FGHD, The Positive Gang*

Zachary Rook, Australia
www.yourlocalmovers.com.au
Moving & Storage
Director of *Your Local Movers*

ABOUT THE AUTHOR & THE GLOBAL YOUTH PROJECT

Entrepreneur. Speaker. Author. Champion of Youth. Joan has combined decades of experience and knowledge delivering her *Programs for Peak Performance* in numerous countries around the globe with both her success in the business world and the lessons learned from her extensive travels and adventure to form the Global Youth Project. The GYP was created to inspire, enliven, educate, and empower as many young people as possible to become courageous, confident goal achievers.

To find out more about Joan's programs or to inquire about hiring her as a speaker or trainer, please contact her through the Global Youth Project, *www.globalyouthproject.org*.

BIBLIOGRAPHY

CHAPTER ONE
Nightingale, Earl. *The Strangest Secret*, 1956.

Sagan, Carl. *Cosmos*. United States: Random House, 1980.

Kaufman, Nikki, *Normal*. https://nrml.com *with permission.*

CHAPTER TWO
Johnson, Cameron. *You Call the Shots*. New York: Free Press, 2007 *with permission from the author.*

Jobs, Steve. Stanford University, *Commencement Address* June 12, 2005.

Young, Scott. www.thebartendingmasters.com/meet-the-experts/scott-young *with permission*

Gates, Bill. Interview – Academy of Achievement (March 17, 2010). Retrieved March 25, 2015 from www.achievement.org/autodoc/page/gat0int-1

Nightingale, Earl. *The Strangest Secret Article*. NightingaleConant. Retrieved June 19, 2015 from www.nightingale.com/articles/the-strangest-secret

CHAPTER THREE
Behrend, Genevieve. *Your Invisible Power*, Massachusetts: The Elizabeth Towne Co. Inc., 1921.

Gretzky, Wayne. *Gretzky: An Autobiography*. HarperCollins, 1990.

CHAPTER FOUR
Hill, Napoleon. *Think & Grow Rich*. Ballantine Books, 1988.

Doherty, Fraser. *SuperBusiness*. Capstone Publishing Ltd., UK, 2011 *with permission from the author.*

Olmos, Edward James – Executive Producer. *Lives in Hazard*. USA, 1994.

Mullen, Siobhan. Article by Bramwell Ryan – "Rising Star," *Canadian Living Magazine*, October 1994 issue.

Pulos, Dr. Lee, PhD. *Beyond Hypnosis*. San Francisco, Omega Press, 1990.

Helmstetter, Shad. *What to Say When You Talk to Yourself*. NY, Pocket Books, 1987.

Eker, T. Harv. Facebook quote, Public Figure page, March 2, 2012. www.facebook.com/HarvEker/posts/10150654971418390

BIBLIOGRAPHY (CONT'D)

CHAPTER FIVE

Graham, Martha. *The Life and Work of Martha Graham*, by Agnes de Mille. Random House, 1991.

Bilanich, Bud, Ed.D., The Common Sense Guy. http://www.budbilanich.com/

CHAPTER SIX

Yanni. *Yanni Live at the Acropolis*, with The Royal Philharmonic Concert Orchestra, VHS, Private, Inc. & Yanni, Inc. 1994.

CHAPTER SEVEN

Frankl, Viktor. *Man's Search for Meaning*. Massachusetts, Pocket Books, 1984.

CHAPTER EIGHT

Hadfield, Chris. Article by Jill Buchner in *Canadian Living Magazine*, May 2015.

NASA references: www.nasa.gov/mission_pages/station/expeditions/expedition30/tryanny.html Retrieved March 25, 2015.

Hill, Napoleon. *Think & Grow Rich*. Ballantine Books, 1988.

CHAPTER NINE

Dyer, Dr. Wayne W. Post to his Facebook page, December 16, 2014 www.facebook.com/drwaynedyer/photos/pb.83636976029.-2207520000.1434768867./10152901116211030/?type=3&theater

CHAPTER TEN

Laszlo Bock, *New York Times* article. "How to Get a Job at Google," writer Thomas L. Friedman, February 2014.

Schuller, Robert H. *Success Is Never Ending, Failure Is Never Final*. Bantam Books, 1988.

King, Dr. Martin Luther, Jr. MLK Quote of the Week: Faith Is Taking the First Step, February, 2013. www.thekingcenter.org/blog/mlk-quote-week-faith-taking-first-step

GLOBAL youth PROJECT.ORG

EST. 2014

inspire + enliven + educate + empower

Do you have a youth success story to tell?
We'd love to hear from you.
The GYP is a hub for a growing community
of youth who seek to make a difference in their life
and in the lives of others. Let's stay in touch!

Visit us at www.globalyouthproject.org
for additional resources to help you
decide, believe, and begin to live your best life.

Printed in Great Britain
by Amazon.co.uk, Ltd.,
Marston Gate.